PRAY THIS WAY

An Exposition of The Lord's Prayer

by

LARRY A. VOLD

3Crosses

20600 John Drive

Castro Valley, California 94544

www.3crosses.org

Pray This Way/Dr. Larry A. Vold — 1st ed.

ISBN-13: 978-1540708892

CreateSpace Independent Publishing Platform, N. Charleston, SC

DEDICATION

This book is dedicated to those people God has used to forge a deeper passion in my heart to be a man of prayer.

To my parents who taught me as a young boy to have daily conversation with Jesus.

To my youth pastor, Myles Gentzkow, who challenged me as a young believer and emerging leader, to spend time alone with God daily in prayer and Scripture reading.

To friends and colleagues in my life who have set aside time to pray with me and for me.

To my wife Carla whom I have prayed with more than any person in my life.

To the Father of our Lord Jesus Christ, who has always been faithful in answering my prayers in accordance with His will.

CONTENTS

ACKNOWLEDGEMENTS 7

INTRODUCTION 9

CELEBRATE HIS INVITATION 13

PROCLAIM HIS GLORY 37

DESIRE HIS REIGN 55

DO HIS WILL 79

TRUST HIS PROVISION 101

EMBRACE HIS MERCY 121

RELY ON HIS PROTECTION 141

PRAYER FOR EVERY SEASON 159

ABOUT DR. LARRY VOLD 179

ACKNOWLEDGEMENTS

There is no accomplishment in ministry that occurs without the help of others. This book is no exception. I'm grateful for the Lord Jesus Christ who has given me a growing passion to pray as He instructed.

I'm indebted to the writers of Scripture who were inspired by God to write about and illustrate by their own example, the power and purpose of prayer.

I'm thankful for other writers who have broadened my understanding of this prayer and aided in my preparation for both the sermon series and this book: Ken Hemphill (*The Prayer of Jesus*), William J. Carl (*The Lord's Prayer for Today*), N.T. Wright (*The Lord and His Prayer*), John Ortberg (*The Lord's Prayer*), R.T. Kendall (*The Lord's Prayer*), Patrick Vaughan (*The Lord's Prayer*), Andrew Murray (*Lord, Teach Us To Pray*), John Dominic (*The Greatest Prayer*) and R.C. Sproul (*The Prayer of the Lord*).

I'm grateful for the encouragement of my editor, Rick Chavez, throughout this project.

I appreciate my ministry assistant, Mrs. Tracy Teyler, whose proofreading skills are unsurpassed.

Finally, I'm indebted to the congregation of 3Crosses for welcoming the teaching series that helped form this book and for putting into practice what they have learned to the glory and praise of God.

"This is the confidence we have in approaching God: that if we ask anything according to his will, he hears us. And if we know that he hears us—whatever we ask—we know that we have what we asked of him." 1 John 5:14-15

INTRODUCTION

"One day Jesus was praying in a certain place.
When he finished, one of his disciples said to him, 'Lord, teach
us to pray...'"
Luke 11:1

It felt like the middle of the night. The room where I was sleeping was unfamiliar and when the largest rat I've ever seen came into the moonlight of a window sill across the room, I decided to spring out of bed in hopes I was only dreaming. As I stood up and took a breath of the cool night air, I realized I wasn't dreaming. The rat was crawling out of the window and now I was wide awake. I decided to find another room where I might read and perhaps get sleepy again.

This was my second trip into mainland China. This trip was intended to give me and my dear friend and colleague, Mark Teyler, a better understanding of the underground church — how it operated — and to witness first-hand what its leaders and members valued. Through our ministry partnership at the time, we were given the opportunity to join a training session in a secret location that would reduce the risk of being discovered by government officials. This covert operation was taking place at a senior center where forty church planting pastors would meet with us for a few days in very tight quarters to learn from each other. It was the first night of our gathering after a long day of training.

I looked at my watch. It was 4:00 a.m. As I walked down a hall toward a room I had passed earlier in the afternoon thinking I might find some privacy there, I was surprised to hear a murmur of voices as I approached. Rounding the corner, I was shocked to see this group of pastors already up, dressed, crouched down on hands and knees, all praying aloud softly.

I stopped in my tracks. These pastors were praying! At 4:00 a.m.? I wondered when they had actually started this prayer meeting? Many had tears coming down their cheeks. Several only wept as they prayed silently. Some were clustered together in smaller groups. I sat down and observed from the corner of the room. How long would they pray? I opened my Bible and started reading. I offered my own intercession. After an hour I was finished but these pastors were just warming up. 5:00 a.m.....6:00 a.m.....I was exhausted and went back to my room to try and get just another hour of sleep to offset my jet-lagged body. As I lay down, I could faintly hear their sweet and gentle murmur of prayers being lifted like incense to God.

I've never forgotten that early morning prayer meeting. It's a reminder to me about the primacy of prayer for any of God's servants. The question that I began wrestling with that day is one that comes to mind often: Do I pray as I ought to? I have to admit that, while my prayer life has grown since that day nearly 20 years ago, I feel there is so much still to learn and apply. I've also learned that the greatest way to learn how to pray is simply to do it more often. Prayer is something that every believer can practice and this is what motivated me a few years ago to bring a teaching series on prayer to 3Crosses where I serve as pastor. I first considered making it a topical series, but decided to use one specific text throughout the series. After observing Jesus in prayer the disciples one day asked him to teach them how to pray. His instruction comprises five verses of Scripture. Fifty-two words. This was Jesus' response to the disciples request to teach them how to pray. I felt this was a good place to camp out with our people for several weeks.

This book is a sermonic exposition of the teaching of Jesus known as "The Lord's Prayer," adapted from the sermon series offered to the congregation of 3Crosses in the Spring of 2012. It's designed to simply explain and illustrate the meaning of this prayer and how it should be used to frame the prayers we offer to God each day. While there is nothing wrong with reciting it verbatim as a prayer of our own, it is the writer's conviction that it was originally intended to be an instructional guide for *how*, not *what* one should pray.

This book may be used for personal growth and enrichment, or as material to share in a small group setting.

It is my hope that it will deepen the reader's understanding of not only how to pray, but incentivize one's own passion to pray more. May you be blessed as you learn and apply what is found on the pages that follow.

1

CELEBRATE HIS INVITATION
"Our Father in Heaven..."
Matthew 6:9

I love the game of basketball and, like most fans of the game, I have a favorite player. I began following Stephen Curry when he played with the Davidson Wildcats from 2006 to 2009. Curry, who became the seventh overall pick for the Golden State Warriors in 2009, was scheduled to be a featured guest at a promotional event put on by a sports memorabilia store near our home. This was, of course, before he became a two-time MVP in the process of demolishing the NBA's 3-point shooting records. My daughter purchased a ticket for me to receive an autographed Steph Curry picture in person and the day of his scheduled visit had finally arrived. I couldn't wait to meet him so I showed up at the location thinking I was early, only to discover that more than a hundred people had already arrived before me. So I waited in line with the others, mostly kids with their parents, looking forward to spending a few seconds with a superstar basketball player. After waiting for what seemed like forever, it was finally my turn to meet him so I stepped forward.

My voice quivering a little, I began, "Hey, Steph, just want you to know I think you're the best ball player I've ever watched play the game!" I continued…"and I appreciate the kind of person you are both on and off the court."

By this time, I could feel the line pressing in behind me with people probably thinking, "Keep it moving buddy…cut the chatter!"

He finished signing his picture as I added, "I pray for you and your testimony as a Christ follower."

He looked up. "Really? Thanks, man. I appreciate that."

He quickly took the photo he'd just signed out of my hand and scribbled out Philippians 1:21 below his signature, handing it back to me with a smile. That photo, along with his signature and Scripture citation sits atop the bookshelf in my office, reminding me of the day I got to actually talk to my basketball hero, Steph Curry.

It's easy to be enamored by people who carry celebrity status. If you've ever had the chance to speak to someone truly famous, you probably know what I mean. We find ourselves thinking, "Will I say the right thing? Will I sound like a crazy person?" The two things I remember most about that brief encounter was how nervous I was to actually say something meaningful to Steph and how the mention of prayer got his attention.

Did you know that the God of the Universe invites us to have conversation with Him anytime we desire? How do you feel about this? Do you get excited knowing you can speak with God? Or, does it make you nervous? Do you fear saying something that might come out wrong or make you sound a little crazy? Do you believe God actually listens when you speak to Him? Do you hold a suspicion that perhaps you aren't the kind of person God pays much attention to? These are just a few of the reasons some of us pause before accepting God's invitation to come and have a conversation with Him.

But did you know that God welcomes and even invites us to talk to Him anytime and anywhere? Did you know that there is a simple pattern that can guide us into a beautiful conversation with our Creator any time we come to Him?

Pray This Way is a close look at the most well-known prayer in the Bible, a prayer the Lord Jesus taught His disciples. We who are Protestant call it "The Lord's Prayer" or, in more recent times, "The Disciples' Prayer," since Jesus was never heard actually reciting this prayer. If you have a Catholic background, you know it as "The Our Father." More people in the world have heard of, recited and prayed this prayer than any other prayer recorded in Scripture.

The first century document known as the Didache or "the apostle's teaching," taught believers to pray this prayer three times a day and every time a group gathered for worship. We don't hold the Didache as authoritative as we do the Canon of Scripture, but it is interesting to note how the earliest believers viewed this prayer. Further, the Didache spelled out that only after a believer had been baptized was he or she qualified to recite The Lord's Prayer. Having the right to recite The Lord's Prayer was viewed along the lines of partaking in communion by many in the first few centuries of the early church — it was only for believers and was not to be encouraged among those outside of faith. Believers were taught to pray this prayer daily as a reminder of their relationship to others in the body of Christ. Nevertheless, the prayer that Jesus taught His disciples is a prayer that can teach us how to pray today.

Prayer seems to be a difficult discipline for many of us. We know how important it is for our own growth and for God's purposes to be accomplished, yet many of us have never cultivated a consistent and compelling prayer life. We let others pray but we hold back. There's a stigma that prayer is only for professionals like pastors, elders, teachers and small group leaders. For some of us, our biggest fear is that someone would ask us to pray publicly! I've been in groups that allow for a time of prayer and, after a long period of silence, the leader just closes in prayer. I can almost guarantee that if I'm at some gathering where believers are and someone is asked to pray, it will be me. Can't anyone who knows Jesus pray? Do we need to be a pastor or church leader to pray in an appropriate manner? Many would answer that question with a resounding "Yes." I believe Jesus' answer would be a resounding "No."

If our fear isn't praying publicly, it's praying ineffectively. Many of us struggle with knowing how to pray.

For some reason, for many of us, talking to God is intimidating. Can we just tell Him what is on our heart? Are we asking for the right things? What if I ask and God doesn't give me what I'm asking for? Does that mean I'm not praying correctly? Is prayer a formula that, when we get it right, we get what we are asking for? Some people might wrongly assume that praying with just the right words or in just the right way will give them riches or fame. This, of course, isn't why God invites us to come and talk to Him. Prayer, for some of us, is not easy to understand at all.

So that's the reason for this book. We want to raise our confidence in God's promise that "we can approach the throne of grace with confidence, so that we may receive mercy and find grace to help us in our time of need" (Hebrews 4:16). We want to learn that, while we don't always know what to pray for, "the Spirit of God intercedes for us as we pray in accordance with God's will" (Rom. 8:26-27). We want to deepen our conviction that God invites us to pray and loves it when we do.

As I thought about how we could learn more about how to pray, I felt the best place would be learning from what Jesus revealed to us in the most familiar prayer found in Scripture. There are six petitions in this prayer and each chapter in this book will focus on one. We will begin by looking at the first phrase, which is not a petition, but the opening address that Jesus taught us to use when we pray. As a starting point, let's read through this prayer as Jesus taught His disciples:

"This, then, is how you should pray: "'Our Father in heaven, hallowed be your name, your kingdom come, your will be done, on earth as it is in heaven. Give us today our daily bread. And forgive us our debts, as we also have forgiven our debtors. And lead us not into temptation, but deliver us from the evil one" (Matthew 6:9-13).

Did you notice that the first three petitions in this prayer are all about God? Prayer begins with our focus on God. His name, His kingdom and His will are to be our first focus in prayer. Then, our personal needs follow. Our need for bread. Our need for forgiveness. Our need for spiritual protection. First God, then us. I think we all have a tendency for our prayers to be simply asking for things.

"God, I need a job."

"God, please give me peace."

"God, do something about my husband!"

Not that these are inappropriate requests, but our focus is often first on ourselves and our needs. Jesus' instruction on how to pray begins with putting our focus on God first, not our needs. This is where our prayers must begin. Wouldn't it be disconcerting if a friend or someone close to you always began their conversation with you by asking for something?

"Larry, I need your car."

"Larry, I need your time."

"Larry, I need your help."

As nice as it is to be needed, this would likely get old real fast. No one likes feeling as if a relationship is based solely on what one person can do for the other. Relationships are built on a mutuality of giving and receiving and I think this is true of our relationship with God. As much as He invites us to ask for what we need, He instructs us to begin with a certain focus on His nature and character. He's inviting us to know Him, not just to use Him for our own purposes. Otherwise, prayer might be compared to putting money in a vending machine and waiting for what we want to pop out. That's not how prayer works.

Notice also in the prayer that Jesus taught us the use of pronouns. Not "My Father" but "Our Father." Not "Give me my daily bread" but "Give us our daily bread" and so on. The use of pronouns is significant and we'll be returning to that often throughout our examination of this amazing prayer. So let's get started. First, I'd like to point out four things worth considering if you want to pray the way Jesus taught His disciples.

THE INSTRUCTION

In Matthew 6:9, Jesus introduces His instruction on prayer by making a comparison. "This, then, is how you should pray" (Matthew 6:9a).

"This, then" refers to the contrast of what we find in the previous section (Matthew 6:5-8) where Jesus points out the wrong way to pray. Praying for public recognition is wrong. Jesus said don't pray to seek recognition from people. Pray this way: go into your room and close the door. There's nothing wrong with public prayer but, fundamentally, prayer is our personal conversation with God. In other words, we don't pray with the goal of impressing others or God. He isn't impressed by our prayers, He just wants to hear from us. So, when we pray to be noticed by others, obviously, God isn't our focus. Jesus instructed us to not pray that way.

In the church I attended as a young boy, I remember hearing prayers during worship services. There were those praying who sounded like they were sitting in a room with God present, pouring out their hearts to Him. Others sounded more like they were speaking to others in the room, with no sense of God being present at all. While I can't ultimately judge their motives, it appeared to me that some were totally focused on God while others were merely focused on the people listening. Being focused on anyone or anything else but the Father when praying is what Jesus was warning us against.

Some also pray thinking that if they add a bunch of words, somehow God is going to hear them better. Babbling on in prayer doesn't help us make a stronger connection with God. Pagans (people who are religious but not in a true relationship with the living God) would often repeat words over and over, as if this would help them be heard. Long, formulaic prayers are popular among some people and religious groups, but they don't cause God to listen to them. So, on the heels of the wrong way to pray, Matthew records Jesus instructing the disciples, "how to pray."

Only Matthew and Luke record this prayer that Jesus taught his disciples and each of them place His teaching in a slightly different context. Luke places Jesus' instruction about prayer on the heels of the question the disciples brought to Him: "Lord, teach us to pray, just as John taught his disciples" (Luke 11:1). It's interesting that, of all the things the disciples could have asked Jesus to teach them, it was prayer they most wanted to learn. Perhaps this was because they witnessed such power and influence from the way Jesus prayed.

I remember hearing the prayers of an elder at our church where I currently pastor and wanting to learn how to pray as he did. Wil Blumert was a man of God whose prayers always seemed so powerful to me. However, what was more powerful was seeing the outcome of his prayers. It seemed that God moved in powerful ways whenever Wil petitioned the Almighty. His ministry as an elder focused on his love for praying for people in our church. Wil's ministry was serving in our prayer room following worship services. He was a true intercessor and, because his prayers were powerful and effective, there were always people lined up wanting him to pray for them. I've met others like Wil over the years, men and women whose prayer life was inspirational in the way they prayed and what happened as a result of their prayers. I spent many hours over the years praying with Wil and having him pray for me and I will always be thankful for his prayers for me and my family.

There's something else of interest in Luke's account of Jesus' teaching on prayer. When Jesus instructs His disciples about prayer, He uses the emphatic verb, "say." In other words, this isn't a casual suggestion. This word gives Jesus' instruction "command form," which is important to keep in mind. It could read this way, "When you pray, you must do it this way" (Luke 11:2a).

It's also worth noting from Matthew's account, the use of the word "how." In Matthew 6:9 Jesus said to His disciples, "This, then, is how you should pray." Notice that Jesus doesn't say, "This, then is what you should pray." In other words, the focus isn't so much on the actual words of our prayers, but on the intent of the prayer itself. So we see this prayer primarily as a model, rather than something we simply recite by rote. There's nothing wrong with reciting it. If it's the way we frame our mind and thoughts so as to know how to pray, and if our hearts are truly engaged in the purest aspects of each of these petitions, that's great. But to simply recite it from memory in hopes that it somehow gets God's attention or is more effective in some way, we are missing the point and are likely not heeding Christ's warning found in Matthew 6:5-8 where vain repetition is condemned.

Some of us went to churches where it was tradition to recite The Lord's Prayer each time the congregation gathered for worship. This can be a beautiful and meaningful expression of prayer when our hearts are truly engaged in what we are saying. But there's a greater chance that, over time, the words can lose their meaning and we find ourselves reciting them without any thought of their meaning at all. This can be like when we are used to driving to a certain place every day and one day, after we arrive, we can't recall a single landmark on the drive itself. Our "auto-pilot" routine didn't allow images we saw to register in our brain. Some of us can relate this to our prayers because after finishing, we can't remember anything we actually said.

AN INVITATION

Now we come once more to the focus of this opening chapter. "Father..." (Matthew 6:9b). One word alone captures the powerful invitation God offers and it's the way He wants to be addressed: "Father." The idea of God inviting us to pray is powerful and compelling. But what is it about the designation of "Father" that makes it a powerful and compelling invitation? I think this invitation captures three important themes:

ADMIRATION

All throughout the Old Testament, whenever God is addressed, He is very rarely given the direct title of "Father." At times He is compared to a father and His nature is fatherly but God's people were more accustomed to give Him names that were far more regal in nature such as Sovereign, Creator, Judge, Holy, Provider, Healer or Savior. The primary name for God in the Old Testament is Yahweh, the name God gave Moses when he asked, "Who shall I say sent me to you?" and God said, tell them, "I AM has sent me to you" (Exodus 3:14).

I AM, translated from the Hebrew verb "to be," led the Hebrew people to come to know their God as the one Who eternally exists. So revered was God's name among His people that no one was to even speak His name for fear that in doing so might somehow be disrespectful. To this day, Jews won't even spell out God's name for fear that in some way it will be irreverent or even blasphemous!

So when Jesus came along in the gospels and addressed God as "Father," this seemed much too intimate, even scandalous. When He instructed His followers to begin their prayers by addressing God as Father, it likely felt the same. How could Jesus be so flippant as to bring Almighty God down to the level of our human understanding? Well, for starters, the intimacy of the Godhead is seen here in this designation and that's why, fundamentally, this title speaks of invitation. Jesus said, pray this way: "Father!" God was Jesus' Father, but for those of us who belong to Jesus, God is OUR father, too! His invitation is based on the intimacy we share in belonging to Him.

As a side note, the Greek word used here is transliterated, "Pater." However, Jesus' native tongue in first century Palestine was Aramaic. The title Jesus most used when praying to God was the Aramaic form, *"Abba."* We would translate *"Abba"* as "Daddy." When a son comes to his father and says, "Hey, Dad, can we talk?" the idiom of *Abba* is used. My kids grew up calling me Daddy or Pop and they still do. I can remember how sweet it was to hear my kids call me "Daddy." I can't recall any time in an informal setting when any of them called me, "Father." For the Jews, "Father" (Greek: *Pater*) would still be too familiar and not nearly respectful enough when addressing God. But Jesus shows by this designation that He is inviting us into intimate relationship. Jesus wants us to come to God like a child comes to his earthly father, in total admiration. Now, I know some of us have had earthly fathers who have not helped us see or appreciate our heavenly Father in this way but this is meant to show us the nature of God as a perfect Father, unlike our imperfect earthly fathers who sometimes hurt us or abandon us emotionally or physically. Jesus noted this contrast between our earthly fathers and our heavenly Father when saying, "If you, then, though you are evil, know how to give good gifts to your children, how much more will your Father in heaven give good gifts to those who ask him" (Matthew 7:11)?

ADOPTION

In the Greco-Roman world, only a father had the legal right of adoption. If a father was awarded an adoption under Roman law, that child was given all the rights and privileges of one born by natural means into a family; legally, there was no difference. Maybe this is why Jesus abandoned His characteristically natural *"Abba"* when teaching his disciples how to address God when coming to Him in prayer. Not only did He want them to come to God as a child admiring his earthly father, He also wanted us to come knowing we have the full rights as sons.

I think this is what Paul was getting at when he wrote to the Galatians: "But when the time had fully come, God sent

His Son, born of a woman, born under law, to redeem those under the law, that we might receive the full rights of sons. Because you are sons, God sent the Spirit of His Son into our hearts, the Spirit who calls out, 'Abba, Father.' So you are no longer a slave, but a son; and since you are a son, God has made you an heir" (Galatians 4:4-7).

I have an adopted sister. Nancy was just a few months old when my parents became her foster parents and were introduced to her through the court system. My parents already had one daughter at the time they were fostering Nancy, but it didn't take long for them to fall in love with her. Soon they were petitioning the court for her adoption.

During that time, my parents welcomed me into the world and, in God's providence, my sister Nancy was eventually legally adopted into our family, too. I don't remember exactly when my siblings and I learned that Nancy was adopted, but I do remember not knowing what the difference was between the three of us.

My parents loved her as they loved me and my oldest sister, Sarah. She was given all the rights and privileges of being raised in our home. No one would have any clue that she wasn't a "Vold" through and through, and when in God's time my parents entered into glory, the inheritance that they had intended for their heirs was distributed in accordance with the law and their wishes. My sister experienced the full privileges (and responsibilities) of our family because of her adoption.

This legal right of adoption and the intimate relationship we share with our heavenly Father is repeated in a slightly different way in Romans: "For you did not receive a spirit that makes you a slave again to fear, but you received the Spirit of sonship. And by Him we cry, 'Abba, Father.' The Spirit Himself testifies with our spirit that we are God's children. How if we are children, then we are heirs — heirs of God and co-heirs with Christ, if indeed we share in His sufferings in order that we may also share in his glory" (Romans 8:15-17).

I love this! Have you been adopted into God's family? If you have surrendered your life to Jesus Christ, you have. None of us are naturally born into God's family. At some point we must intentionally trust in Christ alone for our salvation. It is then that our gracious, loving Father adopts us into His family. In that moment, we become His true son or daughter. How amazing!

ALLEGIANCE

An interesting fact that comes out of the context of Jesus' words is that, in the Greco-Roman culture, Emperor Caesar Augustus was considered the Great Father of the people. He and his subjects all reveled in this. Robert Cornwall, a researcher who studied the political context of

Jesus' day, suggests the possibility that Jesus' invitation for His followers to begin their prayers by addressing God as "Father" might be viewed as subversive, calling them to examine where their true allegiance was, either to the emperor and Rome or to God Himself.

I think this is a beautiful reminder that the invitation from God to come into His presence is punctuated by our admiration, our adoption and our allegiance, and that is all wrapped up in the title, "Father."

OUR IDENTIFICATION

We come now to the first place in this prayer where we notice the plural pronoun, "our."

"Our Father..." (Matthew 6:9).

In the Greek language, the subject, Father, (Greek: *Pater*) stands at the front of the sentence so it reads, literally, "The Father of us..." This sounds awkward in English, so modern translators simply say, "Our Father..."

What stands out through the use of the plural pronoun when addressing God is that nothing in this prayer promotes mere individuality. God is personal, to be sure, but we are not to consider our connection with Him as merely individual. Jesus wants us to see at the outset of this prayer that we have a connection with God which results in our connection to others. We are not alone in our spiritual journey so our prayers are to begin by using the plural pronoun, "Our."

Is this the way we pray? When we come into God's presence, do we stop to realize that while God is inviting us to come to Him personally, we are at the same time coming to Him as a family? We are in community with those who have also pledged their allegiance to God, the Father. While it is important to see this aspect of community at the outset of this prayer, it becomes even more important when we hear Jesus' instruction later on about praying for our needs. We pray in solidarity with all of our brothers and sisters in the world, realizing that all of us share the same basic needs: for bread, for forgiveness and for spiritual protection. We pray with community in mind because we belong to a spiritual family.

I also see here the solidarity we have with Christ. Jesus called God His Father and when we come to God, we call Him our Father, too. Our brother, Jesus, by virtue of His humanity, has passed through the heavens, leading us to the Father.

This indicates that not everyone qualifies to sincerely pray this prayer. Only those related to Jesus and whose Father is God can pray, "Our Father..." You might ask, "Isn't God EVERYONE'S Father? Well, yes and no. He is the Father over all His creation, so in that sense, all people can say God is their Father. But from what we are learning here, the answer is no, not everyone can say God is their Father (See John 8:44). God's true Fatherhood is reserved for those who are "in Christ." This is perhaps why the early believers were

30

protective over who qualified to pray this prayer.

Here is where the gospel invitation comes again. In pointing out the pronoun, "Our," the Spirit of God has room to ask, "Have we made our peace with God?" Is God our heavenly Father? And if He is, then do we not share in each other's lives and with the Lord Jesus Himself? I often hear people describe their relationship with God in the following ways: "It's just me and God; I don't need anyone else. I don't need church and I don't need fellowship. I don't need community." Really? If that is the way someone really thinks, they can never pray as Jesus taught them to pray.

SOME INSPIRATION

I see inspiration in the two words, "...in heaven" (Matthew 6:9b). What I'm getting at here is the motivation that brings us to God in prayer. Many of us don't pray simply because we are not motivated to pray. Sure, in a crisis, EVERYONE is motivated to pray. But Jesus' instruction to His followers about how to pray isn't about praying only during a crisis. What motivates us to pray is knowing that our Father is in heaven. Let me explain. The Greek word for heaven is *uranos*. It is the word from which astronomers named the planet, Uranus. The Greek word is in the plural form so the literal phrase in the Greek language would be: "The Father of us, who is in the heavens..."

Some see in this phrase a reminder of God's transcendence and our distance from Him. There is no doubt that God is transcendent and if we really understood that better, we would appreciate even more that Jesus invites us to start this prayer by saying, "Our Father, who is in heaven." But as true as God's transcendence is, I don't think this is what Jesus had in mind. If this was what He meant, I think the result would be the opposite of what He's going after here; the amazing and sometimes forgotten truth that God desires relationship with His children so He makes himself available, personable and accessible to them.

The phrase, "...in the heavens" could refer to the starry host as we look up from earth on a dark night. Or, it could refer to the atmosphere that surrounds the earth. The question comes down to whether Jesus is intending us to know God's address or whether He is intending us to know His accessibility. God is Spirit, so to say He resides in a particular location is somewhat off the mark. God is omnipresent, meaning he is everywhere at all times. Psalm 139 is a great reminder of this: "Where can I go from Your Spirit? Where can I flee from Your presence? If I go to the heavens, You are there; if I make my bed in the depths, You are there..." (Psalms 139:7-8).

So what is Jesus really saying when he addresses God who is "in heaven?" He is saying that we can be sure that He is as accessible to us as the air we breathe! He's transcendent, but completely accessible, too. This points to the power and compelling nature of God's invitation once more. Some only pray when they go to church. Some only pray when they are in a crisis. But Jesus is teaching us that we can and should pray on all occasions, knowing that God is as close to us as the air we breathe.

This is so beautiful but I wonder if we really understand? Do we come to God with the complete assurance of His accessibility or do we come hoping to get His attention, win His favor, or appease His anger? This is how many people pray; actually, this is probably why many people don't pray as they should. They think their prayers aren't getting through anyway. Jesus wants us to know that when we come to God in prayer He hears us. Why? Because He's accessible. In Hebrew thought, if God could hear His people, they were confident that He would answer. This is why what ancient Israel and even modern day Jews call *"the Shema"* ("to hear", in Hebrew) was the central proclamation of God's people in the Old Testament. "Hear O Israel: The Lord our God, the LORD is one" (Deuteronomy 6:4).

Note what the Apostle John wrote: "This is the confidence we have in approaching God: that if we ask anything according to His will, He hears us. And if we know that he hears us — whatever we ask— we know that we have what we asked of Him" (1 John 5:14-15).

My dad was a thoughtful and caring father. I knew that if I had a need and let him know about it, he would surely do whatever he could to meet that need. My mom was the same. All my life, my parents took care of my needs and even many of my wants. All I had to do was ask. This is infinitely more true of God and His relationship to His children. God invites you and me to come into His presence and talk with Him.

That's why Jesus wants us to know how to pray. He wants us to know we are invited to pray and that if God is our Father, we have full access and rights to Him as sons and daughters. He wants us to come to Him to experience His presence and power. He wants us to know He is as close to us as the air we breathe. He wants us to believe these things when we come to Him. Are we coming to Him this way?

My wife and I raised three amazing girls who are adults now. There's nothing more important to me than when one of them asks, "Dad, can we talk?" There's nothing I'd rather do. God feels this way about us when we come to Him in prayer and if we really believe this, we'd come to Him far more often. Why not spend a few minutes with Him right now?

DISCUSSION QUESTIONS

1. What insight about God might the title "Father" or "Daddy" offer to those who are learning to pray?

2. Identify from the following images which one *best* describes the way you tend to view God when coming to him in prayer: judge presiding in court, high-powered business CEO, police officer or understanding father.

3. Some people find it emotionally difficult to address God, as "Father." Why might this be the case? Even for those who might be troubled by this designation, how does it still provide a helpful and compelling insight into the nature of God and His approachability?

4. How does knowing you are adopted into God's family offer you assurance of accessing Him through prayer? See Romans 8:15-17; Galatians 4:4-7

5. Why do we sometimes feel that God is distant from us when we pray? In what kind of situations are you most inclined to feel God is distant? How does the invitation of Hebrews 4:16 help overturn the suspicion that God is distant or unwilling to listen when we pray to Him?

6. When you pray, how conscious are you of the identity you share with all those who are "in Christ?" How are our prayers enriched by being conscious of this identity?

7. Describe a time when God seemed distant to you. How were your prayers impacted during this time? What

allowed you to return to a more intimate connection with God?

2

PROCLAIM HIS GLORY

"Hallowed be your name..."
Matthew 6:9

Imagine the thrill of being in the presence of a king. As I traveled through Thailand while on a missions trip several years ago, the giant pictures of the late King Bhlumibol Adulyadej (who was alive at the time) were displayed everywhere. Along roadways, in shopping malls and in the lobby of our hotel, the portraits conveyed the loving admiration of the Thai people for their king. I asked our Thai driver if he had ever met the king and he said he had not. I continued, "But if you had the chance, what would you say to him?" He simply replied, "I'd be too nervous to say anything!"

Knowing God is fully accessible and desires us to come to Him is inspiring, but what should we say to Him when we come? The prayer that Jesus taught His disciples contains six petitions. The first three focus on God and the last three on our needs. These petitions provide clear guidelines about what to pray for when entering God's presence and the very first petition is concerned with making God's glory known. We are instructed by Jesus to begin our prayers with a clear focus on the glory of God.

Jesus taught His disciples this prayer so we would know how to pray, not necessarily what to pray for. The how helps determine the what. Keep in mind, Jesus probably didn't intend for His disciples to pray this prayer exclusively. In fact, we don't have any record of Jesus ever actually reciting this prayer, nor do we have any record of the disciples praying it either. It is a beautiful prayer, but it serves as a model for the way we should pray — a template, so to speak — more than simply saying the words recorded here. Of course, there's nothing wrong with praying these exact words if we can consider the meaning of each phrase carefully in order to be more in line with Jesus' instruction for the content of our prayers.

The first petition Jesus teaches His followers is to "hallow" God's name but what does that actually mean? A little boy once heard this prayer recited in the church his family attended. When his Sunday School teacher asked his class if anyone knew God's name, he replied, "That's easy, it's Harold!" The teacher asked him to explain. "We say it every time we pray. 'Our Father who art in heaven, Harold be your name.'" Little children often hear things that are simply not in this prayer. Another young girl's mother once overheard her praying, "Lead us not into temptation but deliver us some email."

Jesus tells us here that God's name is "hallowed," not Harold. But that doesn't explain what it means to hallow

God's name. Most of us don't use the word hallowed very much, if at all. In fact, I can't remember ever hearing anyone call something hallowed. The word hallowed comes from the Greek verb, *hagiazo,* which can be translated as holy, revered or sanctified. Its use depicts the opposite of something that is common.

To use this word when approaching God in prayer is to acknowledge that He's nothing like us. He is completely uncommon in every aspect of His being. In Matthew 6:9, Jesus uses this verb in the imperative mood, which means the petitioner is signifying, not only his understanding of God's uncommonness, but also his own personal desire to exalt the supreme uncommonness of God at the outset of his prayer. Only God is holy in His nature and we are not. It is true that we are made holy by the righteousness of Christ when God saves us but what's in view here is the unique transcendence of God as One who stands above all of humanity and creation. Don't let the picture we painted earlier about God's nearness and accessibility when we pray confuse this point. While it is true that God wants us to see Him as intimately close, we must never confuse His gracious invitation toward intimacy with His complete and uncommon transcendence. We are invited to come to Him whenever we wish, but we are not His equal.

This is the amazing truth we celebrate every time we pray: the transcendent God listens to us! The prophet Isaiah conveys this truth: "For this is what the high and lofty One says — he who lives forever, whose name is holy: 'I live in a high and holy place, but also with him who is contrite and lowly in spirit, to revive the spirit of the lowly and to revive the heart of the contrite" (Isaiah 57:15). In one sense, God is saying He's untouchable but in another, that He's accessible to any who come with a contrite and lowly spirit.

Occasionally, I hear people refer to God as, "the man upstairs." This is an expression that diminishes the awesome grandeur of God's transcendence. Jesus taught His disciples to first come to God by acknowledging His Holiness and our passion to make His glory known to everyone. We don't convey that kind of passion accurately when we refer to God as "the man upstairs." Let me unpack all this a little more by suggesting four ways that praying with God's glory in mind will help us as we pray.

IT WILL FOCUS OUR ATTENTION

The phrase, "hallowed be Your name" helps us get our focus where it needs to be at the beginning of our prayers. When we pray, our focus needs to be on God. Before you start thinking this is too basic, ask yourself whether you typically begin your prayers by thinking more about God or yourself. If you are honest, you will likely admit that your preoccupation and concern has more to do with you than it does with Him. The evidence of this is that most of our prayers start and finish primarily with our needs, our worries and our concerns. We just roll out our grocery list of items and hope that God is listening and will give us what we are asking for. That's often as far as our prayers go.

Instead, Jesus teaches us to begin our prayer by focusing on God. Our first petition, the first request of our hearts should be about God's name being seen as holy. Before we go further, let's take a look at this prayer once more from a little higher vantage point. Notice that the first three petitions have nothing to do with us per se, but only with God. His name, His Kingdom and His will are to be sought after and modeled in this world in the same way they are in heaven. The last three petitions deal with our concerns: our daily bread, our need for forgiveness (and forgiving others) and our need for spiritual protection from our enemy, Satan. So the first half of this prayer is all about God and the last half of the prayer is about our needs and concerns. I think that alone gives us a picture of focus, don't you?

What's wrong with the way many of us pray is that we just don't have our focus on God. When we don't focus on Him first, we don't have much of a chance of hearing from Him with clarity and purpose. It's likely that we'll only hear our own words rattle around in our brains as we speak them. Too many of our prayers feel more like we are just talking to ourselves rather than to God. One day I was in my backyard pruning the roses that border the fence between my neighbor's property and mine. I heard him step out of his back door and after waiting for a moment, I heard him say, "How's it going?" I replied, "I'm doing well. How are you?" No response. Hmmm. Then I heard him say, "Can I come over?" I responded, "Sure, come over now. I'll open the gate." Then I heard him say, "Hold on, my neighbor thinks he's talking to me." I then realized he was on the phone and all the while I thought I was talking to him, but in reality I was just talking to myself. When we pray, sometimes we are just talking to ourselves.

But it is more than just focusing on God that's in view here. It's having a God-entranced vision that Jesus is wanting for His followers. When we gain this kind of vision for God as we pray, we can't help but want others to see Him this way, too. When we say to God, "hallowed be your name," we are simply saying that we know He is holy and we desire others to know Him this way, too.

In the Old Testament, God reveals Himself to Moses on Mt. Horeb. Moses has been in the land of Midian for forty years after leaving Egypt. He's gone from being a son of Pharaoh to being the son-in-law of a shepherd. One day, as Moses was tending his father-in-law's sheep, he notices a strange sight, a bush that burns but is not consumed. He goes to get a closer look and God calls to him from within the bush, "Moses! Moses!" As Moses comes closer, God stops him. "Do not come any closer. Take off your sandals, for the place where you are standing is holy ground" (Exodus 3:5). Moses learns that the God he is being introduced to is holy, something that Moses himself was not, thus removing his shoes was a gesture of humility and contrition. When we say "hallowed be your name," it's like taking off our shoes the way Moses did when standing in God's presence.

When our prayer begins with a sense of God's holiness in view, it also causes us to tread a little more lightly in both the words and the tone of our prayers. We, too, are made aware that God's character is something other than our own and therefore deserves our reverence and respect. This is a great place — the right place — to begin in prayer.

Here's something else to consider. In the same way that the opening address, "Our Father..." causes the one who approaches God to consider whether he has a relationship with God, it does so here as well. We can't say "Father" if God is not our heavenly Father and we can't make it our desire that all peoples would see His holiness if we do not see it ourselves. In this sense, we need our own Mt. Horeb experience where it is clear to us that God is holy and we are not, and our approach to Him requires our own humility. But even for those of us who have come to Him humbly, we are still forgetful of this at times and assume that prayer is more like a magic wand that we can merely wave at the circumstances of our lives. That's not praying the way Jesus taught us; it's more like the superstitious babbling of pagans who hope to somehow appease their gods in order to get what they want.

Consider this question: How long could we remain in prayer if all we did was extol God's holiness? We might run out of words rather quickly. Many of us have not disciplined ourselves to first extol His attributes of holiness when we approach Him in prayer and so it feels uncomfortable. This is something Jesus is inviting us to do: focus first on God's holiness and making His holiness known everywhere.

IT WILL FORGE DEEPER WORSHIP

When we make God's holiness our focus in prayer, we are, in fact, worshiping. Do you consider prayer as an expression of worship? It is! When God is our focus in prayer, our prayers become beautiful worship. We open up and tell God what He is worth to us. That's what worship is, extolling His worth in our lives.

I pointed out that in this prayer the first three petitions are modified by the phrase, "on earth as it is in heaven." So we must hallow God's name as it is being hallowed in heaven. Let's have a look at a couple of scenes where this is seen in Scripture. In Isaiah's prophecy, God gave the prophet a vision of what worship looked like in heaven. What does Isaiah see in this vision? He sees the Lord sitting on a throne, high and exalted, and the train of His robe fills the temple. Above him are angelic figures known as Seraphs (creatures like nothing we have ever seen) who hover over the Lord saying to one another, "Holy, holy, holy is the LORD Almighty; the whole earth is full of his glory" (Isaiah 6:1, 3).

What a scene! The repetition of this refrain three times simply points to emphasis and completeness. God is completely holy. With these loud exclamations, the text tells us that in this heavenly vision the temple doors and thresholds shook. How does Isaiah respond? Does he say, I have a favor to ask of you? Can you give me the winning numbers for the Mega-Millions Lotto? Can you give me a new job? Can you send me a different boss? No, his response is quite different.

He says, "Woe to me! I am ruined! For I am a man of unclean lips, and I live among a people of unclean lips, and my eyes have seen the King, the LORD Almighty" (Isaiah 6:4). This is the proper response when seeing a vision of God. The closer we get to seeing Him as He is, the more we recognize our own sinfulness. It doesn't matter if you were living under the Old Covenant or the New; seeing God for who He is always renders a better understanding of our sinful nature and our need for a heavenly touch. Our commissioning by God to do something for Him often follows moments when God reveals His glory and holiness and our utter sinfulness. Case in point, it is only after Isaiah recognizes his sinfulness compared to God's holiness that God sends him into doing ministry.

In the gospels, after Jesus preached to a crowd while on a beach, he told Peter to put out into deep water for a catch. Peter explains he'd been fishing all night and caught nothing but he will do as Jesus tells him. What followed was a catch so big the boat couldn't hold the fish; other boats came to help but even they began to sink under the weight of the many fish that were pulled from the water. Peter's response to this experience is similar to the prophet Isaiah's encounter with God's holiness in the temple, "Go away from me, Lord; I am a sinful man" (Luke 5:8). Jesus tells him, "'From now on you will catch men.' So they pulled their boats up on shore, left everything and followed him" (Luke 5:11). Peter's commissioning follows a powerful moment of contrition before His Savior.

Forging deeper worship in our lives means, among other things, serving God (Romans 12:1). Worship is simply surrendering to God and prayer is the opening movement that gives way to what God wants in our lives. So, when we pray the way Jesus taught us, we are humbled in the presence of God as we await His instructions. This is a great place to be whenever we come to Him in prayer. I'm recognizing His name as holy and I'm ready to respond. Is this your posture and attitude in prayer?

IT WILL FORTIFY OUR WITNESS

Names have meaning. Some of us might know what our names mean but in biblical times, everyone knew what their names meant. People were named either for the circumstance surrounding their birth or in the hope of something this person might become. I always think of how terrible it would have been to be born to Hosea and his unfaithful wife, Gomer. How would you like your name to mean, "I will no longer show love to the house or Israel?" Or, "You are not my people and I am not your God." These are what the names of Hosea and Gomer's kids meant when they were born. Talk about having a hard time in kindergarten for those two! You think kids made fun of your name?

Names represent two things in Scripture, and even today for that matter: they speak of one's identity and reputation. In other words, our identity is found in our actual names. Our names are found on our driver's licenses, credit cards, passports and on just about anything that properly and legally identifies us. This is why it feels so intrusive to be a victim of identity theft. But the other way names are used speaks of one's reputation. The Proverb says, "A good name is more desirable than great riches" (Proverbs 22:1). Names of celebrities sometimes begin with a reputation that is good, but later turns bad. Sometimes this happens in business. A company with a previously good reputation is smeared by greed at the corporate level. Names mean something.

God's name means something, too. To pray that His name be hallowed is a way of fortifying our witness. We know that our lives and example smudge what people think of God. In fact, looking at this petition a little more closely, the literal translation is, "Let it be hallowed — Your name." In this way, it's a statement of purpose for every believer: "Make your name great through us, by how we live." It's also interesting that the verb Jesus uses is passive. We saw earlier that it is also imperative. This means that we are commanded to want to make God's name great among us, but this is an action that God must do through us. This means that we have to cooperate with Him. If we don't, His name will not be seen as being great through our lives. This is where some of us have trouble. Our lives are saying too loudly things that smear God's reputation. Our actions smudge the name of God and His reputation.

There's a man I've gotten to know at the gym who has a religious background in the Christian Church. Years ago, he decided to walk away from God because of an encounter with someone who claimed to be a worshiper of God, but whose lifestyle completely contradicted his claim. After asking a few more questions about this, I discovered that this disappointment occurred more than 20 years ago! It's amazing how one person's reputation completely devastated this man's view of God and Christianity. I went away from that conversation asking God to help remind this wayward believer not to trust in people more than Christ, and also to protect me from doing anything that might give someone an excuse to walk away from God. When we pray, "hallowed be Your name," we are fortifying our own witness to others.

There are two ways we can do damage to God's reputation. The first is through our words. Remember that God's Ten Commandments include the prohibition against using God's name in vain or misusing it. We tend to think of this as a form of swearing and, while it includes that, it has more to do with using God's name to back up something in our lives that isn't true.

The Jewish people under Rabbinic teaching learned that because God's name was holy, it should never be spoken. There were many names of God given in Scripture, but Jewish people were not to write down these names or speak them out of reverence or fear that someone would erase what they had written and thus desecrate God's name. Even today's Orthodox Jews practice this. They don't write or speak God's name but rather use the designation, "The Name" to refer to God. I don't think this is what God had in mind when prohibiting His people from using His name in vain, but it is interesting when we contrast this to the way most people living in America use God's name.

I wonder what God thinks of all the profanity that is linked to His name or the context of terrible expressions that link God's name to them. I won't be terribly explicit here, but a mild version is the simple way, when being shocked or surprised by something a person might exclaim, "Oh, my God!" Ever hear someone say that? That is a mild form of misusing God's name because when a person says it, it isn't in worship or out of respect for God. It's just an expression void of any real connection to the glory of God. Even Christians are often heard disrespecting God's name by using this seemingly innocent expression.

We can damage God's reputation by our words but even more, we can damage it by the way we live our lives. To live without a desire to pursue holiness in our own lives as Christ-followers leads to hypocrisy when we pray, "Make Your name, Your identity and reputation, be seen as holy through our lives!"

Our dishonesty, our crude and immoral speech, our illicit affairs and our secret sins all chip away at what God wants to reveal of Himself to people who watch our lives. So as we pray, we are, in essence, filtering the way we live, asking God to show us where our lives don't match with what people need to see in Him. Maybe that's why later in this prayer we are taught to pray, "Forgive our sins..." because we are a sinful people.

In fact, it was Martin Luther, the great Catholic reformer of the Protestant reformation, who viewed this petition as more of a statement of repentance than an entreaty of some kind. Luther knew even back then, when we pray this prayer, we would see how unholy our lives really are. So the question isn't whether God's name is holy, because it is, but rather, whether our lives are bearing testimony to this. Praying this way fortifies our witness.

IT WILL FORESEE THE FUTURE

This is probably more of a footnote but I think it is worth stating that when we pray this way, we are envisioning the day when all of humanity bows and confesses Christ as Lord to the glory of God the Father. Paul talks about this in Philippians 2:9-11. It is in that text where we read those amazing words promising that every knee will one day bow and every tongue confess that Jesus Christ is LORD to the glory of God the Father. I see the language of The Lord's Prayer here, don't you? When we proclaim His glory, honor His name and make His name holy in and through our lives, we are simply foreseeing what is in our future when we stand before God in heaven. I think the image here is also that all unregenerate people at the judgment will be compelled to hallow His name; unfortunately, by then it will be too late. This is a picture of Christ's reign and the reminder that one day all will see His sovereign reign. Does everyone see it today? Does everyone you know hallow His name? Hardly. So we pray this way. We pray that the world will see this before it's too late at The Judgment. Have you come to the place where you can say with a sincere heart, "Lord, hallowed be your name?"

"Lord, let your name be seen as great in and through my life, by my words and my actions, so that your name is not tarnished but seen for what it is!"

It's never too late to start praying this way.

DISCUSSION QUESTIONS

1. As you consider the nature of your prayers, how much of your prayers focus on God's glory being revealed compared to your specific requests?

2. When in recent memory have you been overcome with the reality of being in the presence of Almighty God when coming to Him in prayer? What do you feel contributed most to this experience?

3. Have you ever used your prayer time only to extol God's character and glory? Why might this be a helpful exercise for obtaining a more accurate view of yourself?

4. What are things in a believer's life that might cloud people's vision of seeing God's glory?

5. How conscious are you of when God's name is used inappropriately? How have you personally guarded yourself from this practice?

6. As a group, draft a prayer-agenda that reflects the meaning of the first petition, *"Hallowed be your name."* In other words, identify things one might pray for if our concern was that God's name was recognized as holy everywhere.

3

DESIRE HIS REIGN
"Your kingdom come..."
Matthew 6:9-13

The image of a tall skyscraper with smoke billowing out of a large, gaping hole more than halfway to the top of one side filled every TV screen at the gym where I had just begun my morning workout on September 11, 2001. Those who were riding stationary bikes, standing atop stair-steppers or jogging on treadmills seemed to be oddly distracted by what was unfolding before their eyes.

"What's going on here?"

"How could a high rise office building be on fire?"

Then, the unthinkable occurred. From the corner of the image everyone was fixed upon, a commercial airliner entered the scene and flew directly into the south tower of New York City's World Trade Center. The scene was surreal. Suddenly, not just one, but two of the tallest skyscrapers in New York's skyline were ablaze, with certain death and destruction for many people. What was even worse was the morbid reality settling in on the viewers: this was no mere accident. It was intentional. A collective groan could be heard in the room. People stopped what they were doing and many headed for the doors.

That was truly a dark day in American history, and darker still for the people of New York City. Our nation mourned the loss of nearly 3,000 lives that day, with thousands more injured. The ripple effect of that act of terrorism is still being felt in our nation today. The casualties that resulted from the "War on Terror" that followed added to the sorrow of many individuals and families throughout our nation. The struggle and sorrows that existed then still exist today.

It's during these times when people often wonder if the world could ever be a place where sorrow and suffering cease; a world free from evil actions and death. Is that kind of world possible? No matter who you are or where you live there's something in all of us that yearns for a world like that.

This was true for Jesus' disciples, too. Not only was their world filled with the same kind of injustice and tyranny as our own, they were also awaiting a kingdom that had been promised to them as God's people. They were looking for a kingdom whose increase of government and peace would have no end. They were looking for the rule and reign of God, and when Jesus taught His disciples to pray, He taught them to be passionate about seeing this become a reality.

YOUR KINGDOM COME

When Jesus taught His disciples how to pray, He included the importance of praying for God's Kingdom to come and His will to be done on earth as it is in heaven. He taught them to be passionate about asking God to bring His Kingdom to earth.

It's hard to imagine what our world would actually be like if God were physically reigning over it and every person in the world lived in complete submission and obedience to Him. If this were true, it's an understatement to say our world would be a different place. Can you imagine a world where everyone only did good for his neighbor? A world where nations were never in conflict with each other because one sovereign and righteous ruler was over them all? It's difficult to imagine our world this way but in Matthew 6, Jesus wants His followers to envision such a world and to ask for it in prayer.

The prayer that Jesus taught His disciples opens with a beautiful invitation. Whenever we start our prayers by addressing God as our Father, we realize just how accessible and eager He is for us to come to Him in prayer. When we come to Him, there are at least six things, according to Jesus, that should capture our attention as we pray. The first three petitions of this prayer focus on God. The final three focus on our needs.

The second petition in this prayer is, "...Your kingdom come." When we come to God in prayer, Jesus instructs us to ask for God's Kingdom to come. This informs us of what matters to God. We've learned in the previous chapter that

His name matters. Here we learn that His Kingdom matters.
Our prayers should somehow reflect that His Kingdom
matters to us, too. Does it?

If we listen to our prayers, most of us sound more like
we are praying, "My kingdom come..." Our prayers suggest
that we want our rule and reign over our lives.

"God, don't let my boss keep treating me this way."

"God, help my wife to see I have a better idea than
hers."

"God, please do something with my crazy neighbor."

Maybe we don't use these exact words, but our prayers
can sound a lot like we just want God to see our way on a
matter. We are, too often, overly concerned only with the stuff
in our lives and over our relationships, over our little domains
and even the way our world is going. Our human tendency is
to look out only for ourselves. But when Jesus comes and
takes up residency in our hearts, all that changes. Or at least
it ought to. That's why we need to pray the way Jesus taught
us to pray.

One of the keys to understanding these first three
petitions of The Lord's Prayer is to see how they relate to each
other. Most scholars view the phrase, "...on earth as it is in
heaven" as that which modifies each of the first three
petitions. In other words, the rubric or template to understand
exactly what is being said in each of these petitions is to
imagine the way hallowing God's name, His Kingdom rule and

His will being done actually happen in heaven. If we can imagine how these things actually occur in heaven, we have a better chance of seeing how they might work here on earth.

Think about it. There are no competing influences in heaven regarding any of these things. It is only here on earth where we experience the daily, even moment-by-moment, competing influences that hinder God's name being honored, or His Kingdom coming or His will being done in our lives. Considering the way things work in heaven is, therefore, a key to how to pray for those things to happen here on earth today.

Let's take a little closer look at this petition, "...Your kingdom come" so, like the disciples, we can pray the way Jesus taught. I see in this one phrase a few important implications about praying this way.

OUR PROFESSION OF FAITH

Our profession as followers of Jesus implies a present desire for God's Kingdom and rule in our lives and in our world. It would be completely disingenuous to pray this phrase if we were not willing subjects under His kingly rule now. That's why this prayer and, more importantly, this phrase, really can't be prayed sincerely by anyone who isn't yet a Christ follower. This petition alone defines our relationship to the King of the Kingdom and that we are His subjects waiting to carry out His will. Asking for God's

Kingdom to come is nothing short of embracing all of who He is and all of what He desires in our world and in our lives.

Paul reminded the Colossians how, as believers, they had become members of a new kingdom. He writes: "For he has rescued us from the dominion of darkness and brought us into the kingdom of the Son He loves, in whom we have redemption, the forgiveness of sins" (Colossians 1:13-14). Notice that God rescued us from the dominion of darkness and brought us into the Kingdom of the Son He loves. We have been rescued from one kingdom and brought into another. God changed our citizenship. We have a new home.

In my travels to other parts of the world, I've visited places that are politically and ideologically different from the United States. Wherever I've visited, I've observed customs and practices that seem odd to me but that's because I'm the foreigner and I simply don't fit in like I would if I were home. When I visit these places, I'm constantly aware that I'm not home and won't be until I return to American soil.

But that's not completely true either. You see, as much as I feel a sense of being at home when I return from an overseas trip, there is still something that doesn't seem quite right. That's because, as a Christ follower, my true home is heaven. I pledge allegiance to the flag of the United States of America, but my allegiance to America and its political structure is subservient to a much higher allegiance in my life. I have been purchased by Christ's blood and placed in His

Kingdom. Heaven is now my home and that changes everything in my life. I'm grateful for my status as a U.S. citizen, but that doesn't define who I am nor does it determine what my goals or aspirations should be. Don't get me wrong, I can't think of a better country of which to be a citizen, but there is a kingdom that is far more important to me because I belong to Jesus Christ. If you belong to Jesus, God's Kingdom is far more important to you, too. The more we understand this tension, the more fervently and passionately we will pray The Lord's Prayer, knowing that within it we recalibrate where our allegiance belongs.

This is critically important for everything that follows. If you realize as you are reading this, that you are not yet a true citizen of God's Kingdom through faith in Jesus Christ, then neither this, nor what follows in this prayer is going to make much sense. When God transfers us into His Kingdom, a miracle happens. God's Kingdom values get planted in our lives and they begin to grow. "We are new creations" (2 Corinthians 5:17).

That's why everything changes when we are rescued from the dominion of darkness and brought into the Kingdom of Jesus Christ. The changes don't happen overnight because the Kingdom values that we are praying back to God take time to develop. Over time, God builds His Kingdom in our hearts, and through us His kingdom spreads to those around us.

One day Jesus was asked by the Pharisees, "…when the Kingdom of God would come…" and He replied, "The Kingdom of God does not come with your careful observation, nor will people say, 'Here it is,' or 'There it is,' because the Kingdom of God is within you" (Luke 17:20-21). Here Jesus is explaining that the entrance to the Kingdom is an internal matter which will result in external realities. With Christ's incarnation, the Kingdom arrives on earth and, as individuals embrace the King of the Kingdom, the rescue operation is underway. It's still underway today and as it grows in our hearts and multiplies in the hearts of more and more people, God's Kingdom advances.

I've witnessed this in the lives of many people. For many years, I served as a pastor to teenagers in the church where I currently serve as senior pastor. During those years God brought salvation to many teens, rescuing them from the dominion of darkness and bringing them into the Kingdom of His Son, Jesus Christ. Kids begin to understand that God is building His Kingdom in them and wants to spread His reign through their lives. When teenagers get serious about asking God's Kingdom to come on their campus or in their homes, amazing things happen.

I remember a young gal named Vicki who faithfully attended our church. She was a sophomore at a high school that didn't have many other believers but she prayed for God's Kingdom to come to her campus. At our mid-week meeting,

Vicki would often invite one or two unbelieving friends to join her. After experiencing worship, authentic community and the preaching of the gospel in a language that students understand, many of them received the gift of eternal life through Jesus Christ. It wasn't long before she and some of her new believing friends started to reach out to students right on their campus during lunch hour. God's Kingdom came to many of Vicki's friends in her high school simply because she asked for it to come. During my tenure of working with students, I had the privilege of serving alongside many like Vicki.

At the church I attended as a teenager, I experienced this for myself. God brought our church a youth pastor who was excited to introduce God's Kingdom rule to students whose campuses were in proximity to the church. Myles was so passionate about introducing kids to God's Kingdom rule and once that fire was lit, it started to spread. During my four years of high school, hundreds of students from at least five high school campuses near our church were introduced to the gospel of Jesus Christ and many were saved. Dozens were called into vocational ministry, I being just one. Witnessing God's peace and love through Jesus enter the hearts of my peers captured my own heart for ministry. One night, in the quiet of a dimly lit room at our church, I sensed the call of God to bring His Kingdom work to as many people as I possibly could, for as long as I lived.

The implication of this phrase, "Your Kingdom come…" is that it speaks of our own profession of faith and our sincere desire to see God's Kingdom advance in and through our lives.

OUR PATIENCE IN LIFE

The subject of "the Kingdom of God" is widespread throughout Scripture. There are hundreds of references to the Kingdom of God in the Old Testament and nearly one hundred in the New Testament, most of which we find in the gospels. Sometimes the theme is found in the similar phrase specific to the New Testament writers, "The Kingdom of heaven."

In summary form, the simple definition of the Kingdom of God is simply the reign or rule of God. In the Old Testament, God's Kingdom people, Israel, were to be Kingdom bearers amidst the pagan peoples and nations of the world. Of course, the degree to which this took place was only partial and the hope of God's people turned to the anticipation of Messiah who would come to earth and set up His Kingdom on earth where His Kingdom rule would be experienced among the nations. Israel anxiously awaited that day, holding on to prophecies like we find in Isaiah 9:6-7, which speak of Messiah's everlasting government and rule of peace the world over.

When Jesus arrived with the announcement of the Kingdom there was an instant anticipation of Rome being overthrown and Israel regaining its rightful place on the map of the world. Of course, in God's sovereign plan, the kingdom that was being announced was to come in stages. Christ's first coming would usher in a spiritual kingdom that would lead up to an actual physical rule on earth at His second coming. In other words, when Jesus arrived, there would be a kingdom every bit as real and dynamic as the physical rule of an earthly king, but just not as complete. Christ reigns today in heaven over the spiritual kingdom of all those who belong to Him but His people are still awaiting complete fulfillment of all of Scriptures claim and promise for His kingly rule. This is the tension of the New Testament's teaching about the nature of the Kingdom, found in the terms, "already" and "not yet." These are the realities of Kingdom life. It has arrived, but its fulfillment has not yet taken place.

Let's take a look at a couple of references in Scripture that will help us see this more clearly. In the Apostle Paul's first letter to the Corinthians he talks about the order of the resurrection leading up the culmination of Christ's second coming. From this text, we see the anticipation of the "not yet" being fulfilled one day at Christ's return. "But each in his own turn: Christ, the first fruits; then, when He comes, those who belong to Him. Then the end will come, when He hands over the Kingdom to God the Father after he has destroyed all dominion, authority and power. For He must reign until he has put all His enemies under His feet. The last enemy to be destroyed is death..." (1 Corinthians 15:23-26a).

I officiate at funerals frequently. For myself and those who attend, there is a clear reminder that at the present time, death is still waging war on humanity. The obituary page in my newspaper bears witness of this, too. You have probably experienced the loss of a loved one at some point, perhaps even recently. But when God's Kingdom arrives fully, the last enemy will be destroyed. There will be no more death! That's something all of us are looking forward to but we're not there yet. Not even close.

Thankfully, there can be victory over death through the spiritual reality of God's Kingdom reign in our lives presently. Jesus said that when we believe, we "cross over from death to life" (John 5:24). He also promised that anyone who believes in Him would live even if he dies (John 11:25). I once heard someone ask a friend what they hoped would be said of him at his funeral. The person said, "I hope someone says, Look, he's moving." We like to joke about escaping death, of beating the odds. No one wants to die but Jesus promises to any who have faith in Him that in a spiritual sense, they will escape death (John 11:26).

The writer of Hebrews senses this tension of the "already" and the "not yet" as well. In referencing the place humanity will have in the Kingdom that is coming, he writes, "In putting everything under him, God left nothing that is not subject to him. Yet at present we do not see everything subject to him" (Hebrews 2:8). According to the writer of Hebrews, we're not there yet. The fullness or completion of God's Kingdom reign is still in the future. We all see this world aching in sorrow and pain, but juxtaposed is our hope and joy in the promises of God.

So when we pray this phrase, we are saying along with the Apostle Paul, "Lord, Jesus come" (1 Corinthians 16:23)! We echo the very words of the Apostle John, "Amen. Come, Lord Jesus" (Revelation 22:20). We cry out for the culmination of the ages. We resonate with the words of the Apostle Peter, "And we have the word of the prophets made more certain, and you will do well to pay attention to it, as to a light shining in a dark place, until the day dawns and the morning star rises in your hearts" (2 Peter 1:19).

Once again, the Apostle Paul zeroes in on this tension in his letter to the Romans: "We know that the whole creation has been groaning as in the pains of childbirth right up to the present time. Not only so, but we ourselves, who have the first fruits of the Spirit, groan inwardly as we wait eagerly for our adoption as sons, the redemption of our bodies. For in this hope we were saved. But hope that is seen is no hope at all. Who hopes for what he already has? But if we hope for what we do not yet have, we wait for it patiently" (Romans 8:22-25).

That's what we are doing right now. We are waiting, and while we wait, we groan inwardly. There's something deep inside that tells us that someday things will be different. Better. We know that all the wrongs will be made right and that our pain and suffering in this life will be over. That our physical bodies, racked with sickness and disease will be transformed in the likeness of Christ's resurrection body. We know our world will be different. So we wait. Praying this phrase implies not only the truth of our profession of faith, but also our patience in waiting for its fruition.

OUR ULTIMATE PURSUIT

When they come to this little phrase, people who pray this prayer sincerely are reorienting their focus toward Kingdom priorities. When we come to Christ, our personal kingdom topples. The Apostle Paul writes, "I have been crucified with Christ so that I no longer live but Christ lives through me (Galatians 2:20). Our primary objective as followers of Jesus Christ is to knock down any present kingdom in our hearts that stands in opposition to His. We pursue a life that reflects the kingly rule of God in our hearts daily, knowing that we are never more alive, at peace, effective, fruitful, joyous and satisfied than when we seek the Kingdom of God first.

The Sermon on the Mount is the charter for life in the Kingdom. Jesus says to those who are prone to pursue even the basic needs of life to "...seek first His Kingdom and His righteousness, and all these things will be given to you as well" (Matthew 6:33). Jesus says, in essence, that we need a constant reorientation toward the Kingdom in our lives, otherwise we are overtaken by lesser causes and kingdoms that do nothing but rob us of our joy and satisfaction in Him. Many of us are missing out on so much because we are not praying this way; we are not saying, "Your Kingdom come" into my heart, life, family, vocation, finances, relationships, identity and everything else.

If there are compartments in our lives that we've not given God access to, we can't possibly pray this phrase with sincerity. Yet many of us ask God's Kingdom to come into our relationships at home, but continue to belittle each other with unkind words. We ask God's Kingdom to come in our workplace, but we continue to show up late or talk disrespectfully to our boss or coworkers. We ask God's Kingdom to come in our finances, but we refuse to support His work. It's like we are spiritually schizophrenic, asking God for His Kingdom to arrive in some area of our lives and then avoiding or even resisting His promptings for us to join Him there.

My niece and her husband evidenced their understanding of this prayer when deciding to purchase their first home. Lauren and Peter are strong believers who decided that God wanted them to locate to the inner city even though they had the resources to live in the suburbs. Their modest home has been a strong ministry post to reach out to neighbors and friends in a community that needs Jesus Christ. They purposefully look for ways to touch others with the love of Jesus Christ and model this kind of life to their three growing children. Every time I visit them, I'm touched by the stories I hear of their intentional witness to show and share the love of Jesus Christ in their neighborhood. There in that little community, God's Kingdom is coming. That's what happens when God's people pray that His Kingdom would come!

I have dear friends whose dream was to live in a home that could be used to help people find Sabbath rest amidst life's challenges. This had been their prayer for several years through developing their business, changing careers and raising four kids in a very populated area of the East Bay. They were very involved in our church and led a blended families Bible Study. Vince and Delna's prayer was answered when God opened the door for them to move to Eldorado Hills, to a beautiful and spacious home on a piece of property that is perfect for their ministry. Their "Be Still Ranch" is dedicated to helping people find rest and rejuvenation as they sit quietly before the Lord, which has resulted in God's Kingdom coming in new and fresh ways to people and places all over Northern California. That's what happens when God's people pray that His Kingdom would come!

Asking for God's Kingdom to come sometimes moves us in an unexpected direction. My friend Alan was a successful engineer who loved adventure. When his home church in San Jose hosted a speaker who served by helping missionaries travel by small aircraft, Alan began sensing that perhaps God was speaking to him. But with a family, a mortgage and a very full life, what might God want him to do? He wondered. He prayed. God eventually redirected Alan's career path and moved him and his family to Africa to fly missionaries from one location to another. Now he serves in a different ministry in the Middle East, equipping churches and leaders to reach the Muslim world for Christ. God's Kingdom is coming to some of the most difficult areas in the world to penetrate with the gospel. How was all of this possible? Alan prayed the way Jesus taught him to pray. That's what happens when God's people pray that His Kingdom will come.

This phrase that Jesus taught us to pray has implications on our profession of faith, our patience when waiting and our pursuits along the way.

OUR EXPERIENCE WITH POWER

It struck me that Jesus offers the key to how Kingdom work begins, continues and finishes in the world. That key is prayer. While we might be looking at this passage from a theological and exegetical standpoint, let's not forget the simplicity of what is going on here. This is a prayer. Jesus is saying, pray this way. Pray, "Your Kingdom come..."

Do we believe that God wants to bring His Kingdom to earth now, even knowing He will eventually do this for all the world to see? Shouldn't we be praying that God would bring heaven's glory and beauty into every part of our lives and society? Could your campus benefit by God's presence being felt more frequently? What would be different about our homes if God's Kingdom arrived through gracious communication and loving acts of service? Or what about work? Would your boss or fellow employees be encouraged if a little bit of heaven showed up more frequently?

There's some big ticket items that should be on our prayer agenda as well. Don't we want to see God's Kingdom deal a crushing blow to problems like human trafficking, homelessness and poverty? Is it possible that God could bring peace to nations in conflict if some leaders might pray earnestly for God's Kingdom to rule and reign when making policies? How do we bring God's Kingdom to a world so dark and filled with such hurt and hatred? Whatever it's going to take, it won't happen without prayer. And it won't happen without prayers that are asking God for His Kingdom to come in the dark corners of our society and world.

If you have a burden for any of the injustices in our world, the first place to begin bringing change is by getting on your knees. God may have you do many things, but not before you pray. Prayer is where it must start. Jesus promised, "I tell you the truth, anyone who has faith in Me will do what I have been doing. He will do even greater things than these, because I am going to the Father. And I will do whatever you ask in My name, so that the Son may bring glory to the Father. You may ask Me for anything in My name, and I will do it" (John 14:12-14). The Apostle James wrote, "The prayer of a righteous man is powerful and effective" (James 5:16).

OUR PARTICIPATION IN TOUCHING THE WORLD

There is no way to pray this part of The Lord's Prayer without wanting in some way to make a difference in the areas of our world where people are hurting and need help. At some point in recent history, the church decided that it wasn't as important to meet the physical needs of those around us as it was to reach their spiritual needs. Some of us wrongly separate physical needs from the spiritual ones. Read what Jesus said in Matthew 25 about what characterized those of His Kingdom and see if you think God doesn't care about people's physical needs.

The gospel requires that words are shared that explain our fallen state and need for forgiveness through Jesus Christ. But when we ignore meeting the needs of those around us, the people we are hoping to reach have a difficult time hearing our words. Words are essential to conveying the message of the gospel but our works pave the way. When we show indifference or, in some cases, demonstrate something negative to others, it's like our lives are speaking so loudly our words can't be heard.

We ought to practice this among ourselves so that it becomes easier when we try to advance the gospel outside of the church. Read the Book of Acts and see a church that knew if it couldn't demonstrate love and care among its own members, it wouldn't have much of a chance among people with no initial interest in God but who needed shelter or a warm meal; or among people who don't have clean water to drink or any way to get medicine; or among people who are dying of AIDS. We need to go there, too. If we practice among ourselves and the needs we see, we'll have a better shot at getting to those who aren't yet saved.

This is where the adventure begins in our lives. When we pray this prayer sincerely, then everywhere we go, we think, "...Your Kingdom come, Lord." Here at the gas station, in the driveway of my home talking to a neighbor, at work or at play. We are Kingdom pray-ers and bearers and the world will see that we bear His image as we give Him our lives and cry out for an opportunity to share His love with others.

Some of us today need to get involved in a cause that we know burdens the heart of God. In virtually all areas of humanitarian needs, there are ministries that welcome people's participation, not just humanitarian. God has a burden for lost people but where are the evangelists? God has a burden for the poor, the hungry, the incarcerated, the vulnerable and those being unjustly treated; the list is endless. If something touches your heart that you know touches God's heart, get involved. Even if it is the person standing in front of you. Let God show you His vision and follow Him.

If you are praying this prayer the way Jesus taught, then you can't not participate. It is implied in the prayer; otherwise we can't (or shouldn't) pray this way.

This phrase in The Lord's Prayer may be the most radical and transformational prayer you will ever pray and it will set you in motion to pray for more things more often, knowing that the world is waiting and needing to see God's Kingdom. We can bring God's Kingdom to someone today. Let's start right here and not stop until the world that we know has seen a glimpse of it. If we do, the world, as we know it, will never be the same.

DISCUSSION QUESTIONS

1. What images or principles come to mind when you think about the phrase, *Kingdom of God?* What images or principles come to mind when you think about the term, *democracy?* What are some of the tensions that exist when we pray for God's Kingdom to come while living in a democracy?

2. When thinking about the future aspect of God's Kingdom, envision a world where everyone and everything is in submission to Almighty God. Do your best to describe this kind of world. Is this the world you are living in today? Is it possible to impact our world with Kingdom values now?

3. What should be the essential aim of those who follow Jesus Christ? (Read Matthew 6:33 and comment.)

4. If we are the instruments that God has chosen to bring His Kingdom to our world at the present time, how might we partner with Him to bring the kingdom of God to: *our church family; our neighborhood and community; our marriages and families; the nations of the world?*

5. What is one area of your life, or sphere of influence that is likely to be most impacted by your desire for God's reign and justice to flow through you to others?

6. As a group, draft a prayer-agenda that reflects the meaning of the second petition, *"Your kingdom come."*

In other words, what kinds of things would one be likely to pray for with God's reign and rule in mind?

4

DO HIS WILL

"Your will be done, on earth as it is in heaven..."
Matthew 6:10b

"My marriage is dying," the young woman said as she sat in my office for the first time. She was trying desperately to hold back tears. "When my husband comes home from work, he hardly even looks at me. He goes straight to the TV and starts channel surfing. It's like I'm invisible. We used to talk about everything but lately, it seems like he's lost all interest." She was only two years into a marriage that had begun losing ground fast. Busy work schedules at first, followed by a series of job changes leading to financial challenges had taken their toll on this newlywed couple.

"Would your husband be willing to go to marital counseling?"

"No, he thinks I'm the one with the problem."

We sat quietly for a moment before I asked, "What are you going to do?" Her response hinted that perhaps others had asked this question only as an entrée for telling her to count her losses and "move on." She looked up at me and with clear sincerity said, "Well I'm going to keep praying and asking God to help us through this because I'm not leaving my marriage. I want to do God's will."

We spent the next thirty minutes or so looking at Scriptures that might bolster her resolve to prayerfully wait on God during this difficult time, along with those that offered instruction about speaking the truth in love and confronting things that needed attention. She left my office feeling more equipped to face her challenge at home with the quiet confidence that honoring God's will for her life was the best option, no matter what the future held.

I wish every appointment I had with someone struggling in a marriage went in that direction. The reality is that far too many people facing a crisis of this kind are only concerned with what they want. But what does God want? Is that question even considered? I'm discovering that for many believers, that question lags behind matters that seem more important, namely what seems right for the person regardless of what God has to say about it.

Jesus wants His followers to be prayerfully aware and intentional about desiring God's will for their lives. When teaching His disciples how to pray, He presented a prayer that, among other things, zeroes in on the importance of seeking the will of God for one's life. For many people, merely reciting this prayer seems good enough. For the many who recite this prayer on a regular basis, my hunch is that very few realize what they are asking for.

In this book, I'm suggesting that, while reciting The Lord's Prayer can certainly be appropriate at times, what's more important is that we let its contents frame what we want to talk to God about. In this way, we can view the prayer Jesus taught His disciples more like a template, or a grid through which we can direct our words and thoughts to God.

With that in mind, we've said that prayer begins by realizing that God has offered us a gracious and personal invitation. The opening phrase, "Our Father in heaven..." gives evidence that the one praying has accepted God's invitation to come to Him as an intimate and loving ally in order to express our heart's desire. God is interested in having us come to Him and wants us to see Him as our heavenly Father; one who is intimate, loving, caring and providing. But we've also said that our prayers should reflect our desire that God's name, identity and reputation be recognized everywhere. We see this in the first petition that Jesus taught His disciples to ask of God: "Hallowed be your name." In the previous chapter, we learned that we should pray with the eager expectation of God's reign over all things and all people. He is our King and we are His subjects. We yearn for a world where our King takes His rightful throne beginning in our hearts and leading to many expressions of service and establishing true justice in the world. So we pray, "Your Kingdom come..."

Now we come to the third petition of this prayer: "Your will be done..." This is big. As a quick reminder, the first half of this prayer is all about God; His name, His reign and His will. Prayer begins with a proper focus on God, not ourselves and our needs. Many of us begin prayer with what we want, but our prayers must begin with a clear focus on God. As we come to this third petition, it should be understood that nothing is more counterintuitive to our human desire for the preservation of self than what we find right here when we say to God, "Your will be done." How should His will be done? On earth as it is in heaven. Many scholars view each of the first three petitions modified by the refrain, "…as it is in heaven." God's name hallowed, His Kingdom purposes reigning and His will being done should all be done in the same way as they are being done in heaven. None of us have visited heaven to actually witness these realities, but it isn't difficult to imagine that each would be done with the perfection and beauty that should compel us to manifest a greater passion in our hearts to see these things in and through our lives here.

Let's take a closer look at the phrase, "Your will be done." It's much easier to recite this phrase by rote than to carry out what it means. I've chosen to frame the meaning of this phrase by stating five challenges that we'll need to press into if we are going to pray this way sincerely. My hope is that you will be able to evaluate with greater precision whether or not this phrase is finding traction in your own prayer life. Here's our first challenge. When we pray that God's will be done, we must not deny how important God's will actually is.

When considering God's will for our lives, allow me to offer a few statements we should rehearse inwardly as we pray:

DON'T DENY HIS WILL

If we are going to pray that God's will be done in our lives, we need to accept that God actually has a will for our lives and that He wants us to find it. Even more, He wants us to do it. In other words, God has an opinion and for Christ followers that opinion is what matters. I'm going to push a little hard here because, while we might agree with this conceptually, there are some of us who live in relative denial of it. If we don't consult God on what His opinion is about something, how can we say with sincerity that we are interested in doing His will? If we aren't letting God rule in our hearts, how can we pray, "Your Kingdom come?" Or, if we are not interested in His name being proclaimed as Sovereign over all, how can we pray, "Hallowed be Your name?" I'm simply reminding us that every phrase in this prayer is a declaration of our profound and complete allegiance to God.

Non-believers deny any sense of needing to know, much less do, God's will. Before God's work of grace begins in our hearts, we quickly reject any notion of submitting our lives to God's will even when we don't yet know what He really wants for us. It is our nature to refuse His will until that time when He opens our eyes through His grace to surrender to Him. Once conversion takes place, God's Spirit works in our lives to search for what God's will is for us. Once we discover what it is and commit to doing it, wholeness and blessing follows. Further, we come to realize that it is futile to resist His will. God spoke through the prophet Isaiah about this very thing.

"I am God, and there is no other; I am God, and there is none like me. I make known the end from the beginning, from ancient times, what is still to come. I say: 'My purpose will stand, and I will do all that I please" (Isaiah 46:10).

It is nothing short of simple wisdom to turn one's life over to the will of God, no matter how difficult it may seem to carry it out. When the Apostle Paul was recounting his conversion experience to the commander of the Roman guard in Jerusalem, he shared the words Ananias gave him that reiterates this truth, too. "The God of our fathers has chosen you to know His will and to see the Righteous One and to hear words from His mouth. You will be His witness to all men of what you have seen and heard. And now what are you waiting for? Get up, be baptized and wash your sins away, calling on His name" (Acts 20:14-16).

Do you notice how Ananias helps Paul discover that God has a will for Paul's life (and for each one of us) and that he should waste no time getting to it? This should be true for each one of us. God's will for our lives is something that demands an immediate response. What is God wanting to do in your life right now? That's something that perhaps God is working on in your heart as you read this book but one thing is for sure. He's intending for you to seek and follow His will. The question is whether or not you understand what His will actually is.

We need to see just how important this is for our lives. To say that God has a will is one of the most basic points we must begin with if we are going to sincerely follow Him. All through His word, whenever a command is offered, a judgment given or an instruction presented, it all points to God having and expressing His will. Let's not forget the most obvious: If Jesus taught us to pray to God, "YOUR WILL be done..." do we need any other proof?

One of the most frequently asked questions that I am asked has to do with how someone can know God's will. Because orthodox Christianity teaches that God's will can be found in Scripture, people are sometimes confused or feel disadvantaged when pondering questions like: "What college does God want me to attend?" "Who should I marry?" "Should I take the promotion at work or stay where I am?" Daily we face questions and decisions that beg the question of whether they are in the fairway of God's will for our lives. So what do we do if the decisions and choices we need to make in life are not necessarily addressed in the Scriptures?

This is a subject that deserves more attention than I can give it here. But let me offer something that I've found helpful for people who seem stumped about knowing what God wants for them when they can't find any Scripture that addresses it directly. It makes sense that if God has an opinion about something, we should be primarily concerned about learning what those things are first and doing them, and not worry so much about issues which are not necessarily answered in the Bible.

For concerns and questions not directly addressed in Scripture, God gives us wisdom to navigate in what seems like uncharted waters. He also uses godly counsel in our lives. Most of all, if we are committed to obeying God's revealed will, I think we have absolute freedom to choose to do whatever we feel is best for our lives, trusting that God will direct us along the way.

What are examples of things that are God's revealed will? Here's a simple example: It's God's will for all believers to be sexually pure. We find this in 1 Thessalonians 4:3 where the Apostle Paul, under inspiration of the Spirit writes, "It is God's will that you should be sanctified: that you should avoid sexual immorality; that each of you should learn to control his own body in a way that is holy and honorable" (1 Thessalonians 4:3-4).

There's nothing ambiguous about this command and he even states the command in the language of it being God's will for us. Therefore, we never have to wonder if being sexually pure and controlling our bodies in a way that is holy and honorable is God's will for our lives.

Following this kind of reasoning, if we are wondering if it is God's will for us to marry the person we are currently dating, but are not honoring God's revealed will for living sexually pure, then it's disingenuous to pray for God's will to be revealed until you have submitted to sexual purity.

It's also God's will that believers be filled with His Spirit. We learn this in Paul's words to the Ephesians, "Don't be foolish, but understand what the Lord's will is. Do not get drunk on wine, which leads to debauchery. Instead, be filled with the Spirit" (Ephesians 5:17-18). Again, we never need to wonder if it is God's will to be filled with His Spirit. We know it is because he emphatically says so. But if we are not submitting to God's will in this area, how can we ask for God's will to be shown to us about whether to take a work promotion or a new job?

Whenever Scripture reveals something that God wants us to pursue, we can rest assured these things are God's will for us. This is important because whenever a believer is hoping to discover God's will for something that His Word may not directly address, the question is whether we are submitted to what God has already revealed. I've found that when we are committed to doing God's revealed will, God does His part in giving us understanding for the things that are not so clear.

DEAL WITH HIS WILL

Things can happen to us that are really difficult, and at times, even tragic. If we are going to pray the way Jesus instructs, we must realize there will be things that come into our lives that we wouldn't have asked for or wanted. Things like 9/11, Hurricane Katrina, a tsunami, tornadoes, cancer, a car accident or any number of difficult things that can happen to us.

When it comes to disasters in this world or disasters in our personal lives, I'm not suggesting that God orchestrated those things to happen. However, because God is Sovereign over all things, we need to embrace the truth that God allows difficult and even tragic things to happen.

Therefore, we are all rightfully repulsed by the religious spokespersons who, in the wake of these kinds of tragedies, show up on TV or radio and with complete confidence announce that these disasters are evidence of God's judgment on a certain people group or set of individuals who are in rebellion to Him. The Bible says there is evil in the world and evil people do evil things. But God isn't necessarily causing these things to happen in order to judge.

We must accept the fact that God allows things to happen that we wouldn't have chosen for ourselves or others. Christians realize that God's Sovereignty allows for things that seem absurd and unnecessary. Perhaps the best biblical example of this is found in Acts and is directly related to

Jesus Himself. "This man (Jesus) was handed over to you by God's set purpose and foreknowledge; and you, with the help of wicked men, put him to death by nailing him to the cross" (Acts 2:23). Who nailed Jesus to the cross? Wicked men did, but not outside God's set purpose and foreknowledge. A shorter version might be the words of Job after losing his entire family and his family enterprise. "The Lord gave and the Lord has taken away; may the name of the Lord be praised" (Job 1:21). It is with this understanding that we pray to God, "Your will be done."

When terrible things happen to us, Christians can pray for God's will to be done because, "We know that in all things God works for the good of those who love him, who have been called according to His purpose" (Romans 8:28). Even when it comes to the tough parts of God's will, we can pray this with integrity and sincerity because we know that He is trustworthy and we can rest knowing this. The Old Testament character Joseph could tell his brothers, "You intended to harm me, but God intended it for good to accomplish what is now being done, the saving of many lives" (Genesis 50:20). Joseph's statement is evidence of his acceptance of God's will for his life, even when it led him far from his family, all the way into Egypt.

Sitting in their home with Anthony and his wife Tiffany in the hours after the death of their infant daughter was a heart-wrenching and desperate moment for all who were gathered there on that warm August morning in 2013. These parents were new believers and, while it appeared that God was restoring and elevating their lives to new heights, the sudden and terrible loss of their little girl could have easily jeopardized their understanding of God's goodness.

I prayed fervently that, over time, God's Spirit would help them accept this terrible loss and not let it become a wedge in their understanding of God's character. Their small group rallied to show them love and compassion. Our church family extended the kind of loving compassion that a family devastated by this kind of loss truly needed. Through it all, Anthony and Tiffany modeled to their children and those who came near to them during this time that they knew God was good and faithful even when going through pain. At their daughter Bella's memorial service, Anthony offered a moving tribute about how he and his wife had a confidence in God's will for their daughter and that this terrible loss had to, in some mysterious way, also be His will for her and for them. While the loss was heartfelt and significant, this beautiful couple demonstrated a prayer language that said in essence, "Father, Your will be done."

Let's introduce one more aspect of why praying for God's will demands we "deal with it." When we are living in ways that are not pleasing to God and doing so without repentance or a desire to know or follow God's will, there is no prayer more appropriate than to ask for God's will to be done in our lives. After failing to repent and follow God's will, consequences show up in our lives because we've ignored His gracious warnings. That is when we need to learn how to say, "Your will be done."

When King David sinned by taking a census of his fighting men, God sent a prophet to pronounce certain judgment on his act of self-reliance. David's response to the prophet was essentially the phrase of the prayer we are looking at in this chapter. He says, "Let us fall into the hands of the LORD, for his mercy is great but do not let me fall into the hands of men" (2 Samuel 24:14). When we can accept the things we see God doing to correct us and discipline our waywardness, we experience an even deeper understanding of praying this way.

Wouldn't it be great if we simply focused more on asking that God's will be done in our lives even when we've drifted from His will in the first place? Perhaps one of the most important action points for us right now is to come back to God's will if we've gotten away from it.

DESIRE HIS WILL

When you ask someone for their opinion, you show them honor. When you desire to know God's will by asking that it be done in your life, you honor God. This is a challenge because getting to know God's will takes time and discipline because the primary source for knowing God's will is learning His Word.

God decided that the way people were to know Him and what He wanted in their lives was to find it in the Scriptures. The Bible is amazing! It's a book filled with the pure revelation of God that can speak into every situation, temptation, problem, concern, dilemma, issue and predicament that comes our way.

As we learned earlier in this chapter, there may not always be a straight line application for the situation we are wondering about, but through narrative, instruction, warnings, rebuke, wisdom and prophecy, the reader is given instruction and illustrations for knowing and doing God's will. We must discipline ourselves to learn God's Word in order to hear and understand what God's will is for our lives. But this takes desire.

God spoke through the prophet Jeremiah: "You will seek me and find me when you seek me with all your heart. I will be found by you declares the Lord" (Jeremiah 29:13-14a). Earlier in the Book of Jeremiah, God speaks through him this way: "Let not the wise man boast of his wisdom or the strong man boast of his strength or the rich man boast of his riches, but let him who boasts boast about this: that he understands and knows me, that I am the LORD, who exercises kindness, justice and righteousness on earth, for in these I delight" (Jeremiah 9:23-24). The words of Jeremiah reflect both our need for desire to seek God's will and the affirmation that comes from God when we do.

We prefer shortcuts when it comes to knowing God's will. We have a microwave mentality about deciphering God's will. We want quick, easy answers to everything. Many of us expect God to reveal everything we need to know about what's going on in our lives in the 30-40 minute message we hear on Sunday. Considering the fact that many evangelicals miss as much as fifty percent of the worship services offered in their local church, don't you think it's expecting a lot from God that all of our questions would be answered in that short time? (Not to mention expecting a lot from your pastor!) Sure, we might listen to a podcast message during the week to supplement our intake of God's Word, but we won't learn very much even by doing that. We need a disciplined and regular study of God's Word, yet so many believers simply never do this.

If we are going to sincerely pray for God's will to be done in our lives, we need to be devouring Scripture. We need to read, meditate, study, memorize and even teach it to others so that we get it deeper into our hearts. Daily we receive a deluge of messages that convey other people's will for our lives. Whatever glimpse of God's will I may have received in my quiet time earlier that morning is quickly confronted. But when we pray this way, "Your will be done," we are elevating

God's desires and plans for our lives over and against all the other messages we receive each day.

I love Psalm 119 and how it elevates the reader's desire to let God's Word lead and direct one's life. "Give me understanding, and I will keep your law and obey it with all my heart. Direct me in the path of your commands, for there I find delight. Turn my heart toward your statutes and not toward selfish gain. Turn my eyes away from worthless things; preserve my life according to your word" (Psalms 119:34-37). Is there any wonder why so many of us are so lost and confused when it comes to knowing and doing God's will? We must desire to know God's will but this takes discipline. Maintaining a daily time in God's Word, making personal notes, journaling, applying what we learn and sharing what we have learned is only the beginning.

I've been a Christ follower since I was in third grade but even before that, I was learning about God through the Bible at home, at church and in Sunday School. My faith began to mature when I was in high school and my calling from God to vocational ministry happened when I was in college. After attending two years at a local junior college I transferred to a Christian liberal arts university where I earned my degree in Biblical studies and Christian Education. Then I earned a Masters degree in Theology and, eventually, a Doctor of Ministry degree. I went to school without taking much of a break until I was 40 years old. I'm educated way beyond my intelligence and do you know what I've learned? Not nearly as much as I should have!

The more you learn from Scripture, the more you realize how much you really don't know. Believe me, I share my educational background more out of embarrassment because I should know way more than I do. Even more importantly, I'm still not applying everything I've learned. Mark Twain once said something along the lines of, "It's not the Bible verses that I don't understand that trouble me; it's the ones I do understand but haven't applied to my life that trouble me most."

Therefore we should never stop learning because we will never arrive at knowing our Savior as He can be known in this life alone. We'll even be learning in eternity, I'm sure of that. God has much to show us. Is it our desire for God's will to be done now and even throughout eternity?

DISCERN HIS WILL

If we are disciplining ourselves to study and meditate on God's Word, we will be planting for a harvest of understanding so we can do God's will. I've been saying throughout this chapter that it is sometime difficult to know exactly what God's will is for our lives. Let's remember what God said through the prophet Isaiah, "For my thoughts are not your thoughts, neither are your ways my ways,' declares the LORD" (Isaiah 55:8). Because God's thoughts are not our thoughts or His ways the same as our ways, we need wisdom and discernment to know God's will. In this vein, we can pray, "God's will be done" in our lives.

In the Old Testament, God's people experienced an occasional "Word" spoken directly by God or one of His prophets. As in the example of Gideon in Judges 6, a fleece was put out to test what God's will was for a specific situation. The priest had the mysterious Urim and Thummim (Numbers 27:21), which most scholars believe were used by the priest in some way to discern God's will for the people. But what about us? What comfort do we have when we are looking for God's will but can't find anything in Scripture to let us know if we are on the right track?

For this, Romans 8:14 is helpful: "...those who are led by the Spirit of God are sons of God." I like that! Turn that around and you could say, "The sons of God are led by God's Spirit." This brings great encouragement to our lives when we are hoping to live in God's will. It's also important to realize that, as we seek God's will through a daily and thorough diet of His Word, we are better equipped to discern the nudges and promptings of the Spirit of God. In other words, it's easy to mistake God's will for a simple and even good desire in our own lives, or for an appetite of our flesh. So we need to be careful and patient when desiring God's will or the confirmation of it in our lives.

This is the beauty of the instrumentality of the Holy Spirit's work in our lives. When we ask for God's will to be done in our lives, while knowing we have searched Scripture to the best of our ability for instruction and confirmation about it, we can be sure to receive assistance from the Spirit to lead and guide our hearts toward the things that God desires for us.

When we pray this way, we are coming before God knowing that he does have a plan and an opinion about what's going on, but we need help knowing what to do. We pray also with a confidence in His Sovereignty that He knows what He is doing, and that even in those terrible situations that arise from the evil world we live in, or from the consequences of our own waywardness or laziness, God is going to work things out. When we pray this way, we are also telling God that we desire to know His will, that we are diligently searching for it, not wanting quick fixes and shortcuts for things that require more time. When we pray this way, we are also asking God to have His way even in spontaneous moments when His leading seems unclear.

DO HIS WILL

When we pray this way, we are saying to God, "Have your way right now or in this situation." We learn this from how Jesus prayed when He was in the garden on the night He was betrayed "Father, if You are willing, take this cup from Me; yet not My will, but Yours be done" (Luke 22:42).

"Do not merely listen to the word, and so deceive yourselves. Do what it says" (James 1:22). It isn't knowing God's will that is most important, it is doing God's will that matters. When you and I ask God, "What is your opinion about this, God?" and when we read it, or hear it, or the Spirit prompts us, and we don't respond with obedience, we are not honoring God nor are we praying as Jesus taught us.

Jesus obeyed His father and did so because He was sincere. "Your will be done." Remember, we are asking that His will be done "...on earth as it is in heaven." If this phrase modifies all of the first three petitions, then we are asking God for His name to be hallowed on earth as it is in heaven. This isn't rocket science. One doesn't have to use much brain power to imagine the way God's will is accomplished in heaven; completely, perfectly and timely! No resistance is anticipated or would be tolerated. So, if you are asking about God's will and He shows you what it is, it should be carried out immediately.

Which of these challenges is the most critical one for you to apply today? You might want to make note of that at your small group or with someone with whom you are working through this material. Secondly, in what specific areas of your life are you seeking to know and apply God's will? There are numerous areas where we need this, but it doesn't happen without genuine attention and intention. Why not begin right now?

DISCUSSION QUESTIONS

1. Tell about a time when you wanted to know God's specific will for your life, or a time when you knew *exactly* what God's will was and whether you did it.

2. When you think about the topic of God's will, which is more difficult for you: Discovering God's will or doing it once you have discovered what it is? Why? Do you have an example of when it was difficult for you to do the will of God?

3. What are some ways to help determine the will of God for our lives? What is the most obvious and available tool for understanding the will of God for our lives?

4. Tell about a time when you experienced a clear conviction of what God's will was for you, though it wasn't revealed directly from Scripture per se. How do you discern if something is God's will for you if it isn't explicitly addressed in Scripture?

5. Look up the following Scriptures and identity the specific action point in each that is in line with God's will: *1 Thessalonians 4:3; Ephesians 5:17-18; 1 Peter 2:15; 1 Peter 4:1-2; 2 Peter 3:9; 1 Thessalonians 5:16-18*

6. As a group, draft a prayer-agenda that reflects the meaning of the third petition, *"Your will be done on earth as it is in heaven."* In other words, what kinds of things would one be likely to pray for when searching for and desiring the will of God?

5

TRUST HIS PROVISION
"Give us this day today our daily bread..."
Matthew 6:11

One of our family traditions while I was growing up
was taking a road trip to the Midwest to visit my
grandparents on their farm in south-central Minnesota. When
we arrived, my sisters and I would jump out of our VW bus as
quickly as we could. The adventures of feeding sheep, chasing
pigs and exploring the musty old barn were just what my
sisters and I needed after being cooped up in the family bus
for three days straight. But of all the memories of our
vacation on the farm, the one that stands out was the Sunday
afternoon family dinner that was served after returning from
the little Grove Lake Church my grandparents attended.

Picture a balmy sunny afternoon with puffy cumulus
clouds and a stiff afternoon breeze. We are all sitting around
the family table that has been set up in the middle of their
country-style farmhouse. Then, out comes my grandma, with
a big basket of freshly baked rolls of bread that are still
steamy hot from the oven. After prayer, I slather butter all
over the soft inside of the roll and gulp it down, followed by
another and then another. I don't remember any of the main
dishes that were served but I do remember the bread! I love

bread and there was no bread as tasty and memorable as my grandmother's when it came fresh out of the oven.

We are learning to pray the way Jesus taught his disciples, using The Lord's Prayer as He intended: as a model prayer for knowing how, not *what*, to pray. The Lord's Prayer is comprised of six petitions; the first three focus on God and the final three focus on our needs. In this chapter, we want to learn what Jesus meant by the simple petition, "Give us today our daily bread" (Matthew 6:11). Jesus is helping us know what it means to pray for our basic needs and it's interesting that the idiom Jesus uses here to represent our basic needs is bread.

I think we can agree that when it comes to comparing our basic urges for satiating our hunger with how we should pray, the picture of receiving bread is an apt one. I realize that in our modern obsessiveness toward healthy diet and nutrition, bread may not be everyone's choice to represent our basic needs. But since the beginning of time, there has always been, in every culture, a basic appreciation for bread as the staple of life and a good representation of the basic things that humans need for survival. Having enough bread comprises the totality of our human needs. When we follow Jesus' instruction that we pray for our daily bread, we are simply admitting that we have needs.

When it comes to praying as Jesus intended, I would like to suggest three specific areas of our relationship with God that this petition helps to bring us face-to-face with.

OUR DEPENDENCY

I see this in the opening phrase of the petition, "Give us…" Jesus wants us to rely, depend and trust in God's provision for every need in life. One of the most important truths to embrace as a believer is that God provides for our needs. When the Apostle Paul wrote to the Philippians, he commended their generous giving during his time of need and gave them the assurance that God would, as a result, meet their needs, too. "And my God will meet all your needs according to His glorious riches in Christ Jesus" (Philippians 4:19).

Commentators point out that the words, "according to" in Paul's promise to the Philippians are words which offer insight into the level of generosity that God demonstrates toward His people. Had Paul merely said that God would meet their needs "out of" his glorious riches, it would not have come close to the impact he intended when choosing the phrase, "according to his glorious riches." To give "out of" one's riches is merely to take a portion of any size.

If someone has a million dollars in his savings account and gives something out of this account, the gift might be as small as a dollar. In other words, to give merely "out of" one's resources, there's nothing especially noteworthy about it. However, if that same person with the million-dollar bank account chooses to give to someone in a manner that is "according" to what he has, that's an entirely different story. That gift would be guaranteed to be sizeable since it was "according to" or "in relationship" to the larger sum. This is God's way of telling us that His resources are plentiful for meeting our needs. God does not give us out of what He has, but according to what He has. This is an amazing reality.

Most of us run into some basic conflict when we set out to depend more on God to meet our needs. First of all, we have a tendency to rely way too much on ourselves. One of the biggest obstacles for making this a sincere petition in our prayers is self-sufficiency. Many of us were taught to only depend on ourselves.

"Be self-reliant!"

"Fix things yourself."

"Take care of yourself."

"Do it for yourself."

"Don't trust anyone."

"God helps those who help themselves."

If we really are only depending on ourselves for the things we have or feel we need, we can't pray this petition with sincerity the way Jesus taught us to.

We need to be careful not to confuse our need to take responsibility with this petition for God to meet our needs.

This petition doesn't give us permission not to work, not be responsible with our time or finances, or create habits that ignore wisdom or planning. But even when we are being responsible and using wisdom to plan well for things, we still must depend on God and recognize that He is our provider. He's the One who ultimately meets our needs. The things that sometimes compete with relying on God are our savings, jobs and material possessions. The list is endless of the things we can depend on rather than depending on God. The petition, "Give us today our daily bread," only takes flight as we recognize God as provider in all things. Relying on ourselves is a hindrance to praying as we should.

I've discovered that as I pray for God to meet my basic needs, I'm far more aware of His provision in my life. I look around and see the many ways God has blessed me and met my needs. I may not always have what I want, but I do have what I need. I could even do with much less in my life and still have plenty. As we pray this petition, Jesus wants us to become more aware of the ways He has provided so that we can share whatever surplus we have with others. If our closets are full of clothes and our pantries full with food, perhaps we should be giving some of it away. We'll see the importance of this a little later in the chapter. But let's consider another obstacle to relying on God for our needs.

Some of us appear to rely too much on government structures or programs to meet our basic needs. If we are not careful, we can start viewing our basic needs as "rights" and before we know it, we are blaming institutions or agencies for not providing as we think they should. There are some who feel that if there are hungry people in our society, the government should take responsibility to feed them. Or, if there are homeless people, the government should take responsibility to house them. Many of us are depending too much on government for things we are commanded to go straight to God about, trusting His provision.

In the political and social context of the gospel narratives, there is something interesting about this petition. For example, when Jesus performed the miracle of feeding 5,000 people along the shores of the Sea of Tiberius (or Galilee), the common reader may not know that Herod Antipas, in his attempt to garner support for the emperorship of Rome, was controlling the bread economy and fishing enterprise around that lake, even renaming it after the Emperor (Tiberius) as a means of putting money in the coffers at Rome. That Jesus multiplied the bread and fish to multitudes on that shore was not only a miraculous statement of how God provides, but also a challenge to everyone regarding whom they should trust for their provision. Herod wanted people to trust the Emperor. Jesus wanted people to trust God. How about us? Is it God or government that you trust to meet your needs?

No doubt this petition of asking God to provide for our daily bread harkens back to the great story of God's provision of bread in the Old Testament. Exodus 16 tells us that in the second month of the Israelites' journey to the Promised Land, they had run out of daily provisions and "...the whole community grumbled against Moses and Aaron, 'If only we had died by the LORD'S hand in Egypt! There we sat around pots of meat and ate all the food we wanted, but you have brought us out into this desert to starve this entire assembly to death'" (Exodus 16:2-3). So what does God do? The text continues, "The LORD said to Moses, 'I will rain down bread from heaven for you. The people are to go out each day and gather enough for that day'" (Exodus 16:4).

When the Israelites asked what it was they were eating, Moses said, "That's what we'll call it: manna!" Manna means, "What is this?" So each morning the people went out to collect manna enough for the day. It was a daily provision. The whole process was miraculous because whatever a person gathered was enough (Exodus 16:18). But here's something even more interesting about manna. It could be boiled, baked or fried, but the one thing you couldn't do with manna was store it. If someone decided to store manna, it would spoil by the next morning. God was teaching the Israelites to depend on Him for their needs. God wanted the Israelites and us to know that the more our capacity to store up for ourselves the greater incentive to trust in our own resources and stop depending on Him for our needs. Nothing wrong with careful planning and hard work, but often our storing becomes hoarding and before we know it, we aren't depending on God to meet our needs.

One of the names God reveals to His people in the Old Testament is Jehovah Jireh (Genesis 22:14), which means, "God provides."

Ken Hemphill, in his book, *"The Prayer of Jesus,"* calls this sense of God's provision, "Father-nature." He writes: "Your Father knows that you have a life. That life includes cereal on the breakfast table, diapers on the baby, a coat on your back, and a pair of decent shoes for your feet. It includes a roof over your head and the money to keep it there, a job to work and the opportunity to excel, a car that runs and a reliable mechanic to help it stay that way. To most people there is nothing spiritual about these things, nothing sacred about writing the check for this month's rent, eating a tuna sandwich, or fixing a leaky faucet. But for us as Christians, these routine matters provide ongoing evidence that a compassionate, loving God cares about the most ordinary matters in our lives."

But when we don't depend on God or see Him as our provider a couple of things are likely to happen. First, we are likely to become stingy. When we feel our resources belong solely to us, we have a difficult time letting go of them. But if we believe God provided all of what we possess, we can

108

release more of it, trusting He will provide more for us if needed.

Another thing that often happens is that we become anxious and worried that what we have worked so hard to provide for ourselves will be gone or that we won't have enough sometime in the future. We need to learn the lesson Jesus taught His disciples as recorded in Matthew 6:25ff: "Therefore I tell you, do not worry about your life, what you will eat or drink; or about your body, what you will wear. Is not life more important than food, and the body more important than clothes? Look at the birds of the air; they do not sow or reap or store away in barns, and yet your heavenly Father feeds them. Are you not much more valuable than they?"

Jesus adds to this illustration by asking his disciples to consider the lilies of the field that do not labor or spin, but not even Solomon in all his splendor was dressed like one of these. Jesus brings up the issue of faith. "Will He not much more clothe you, O you of little faith?" (Matthew 6:30). The disciples' anxiety was due to their questioning of God's ability to provide. It comes down to an issue of faith for all of us. What do we believe about God's provision for our needs?

OUR SERENITY

Fundamentally, this request helps us to evaluate our level of contentment. I like that Jesus focuses his disciples' request for bread rather than, say, lobster. When we pray the way Jesus teaches us, we recognize the difference between our needs and our wants. It isn't that God doesn't sometimes give us what we want, or even more than we need. His grace and provision often gives us far more than what we are even asking for. But He's speaking of our dependence on Him for our basic needs. Asking for bread is a great metaphor for asking God to meet our basic needs and to be content with what we have.

One of the abuses that some people commit when praying is the practice of "naming-and-claiming" things which they believe God wants to give them if they simply ask. Proponents of this view point to verses like James 4:2 where it says "...you do not have because you do not ask God." The rest of that section, however, goes on to say, "When you ask, you do not receive, because you ask with wrong motives, that you may spend what you get on your pleasures" (James 4:3).

I've met people who think that God expects us to ask for wealth and material possessions, and if we have enough faith we will get what we are asking for. This is a twisted aberration of what Jesus is teaching us here in The Lord's Prayer. He didn't say we should ask for bucks. He said we should ask for bread. The metaphor points to God's intent for the nature of our requests.

One thing this petition should do is to help us gain perspective about how much we already have. A while back, the San Francisco Chronicle Parade section featured a new book by Anna Quindlen called, *"Full House,"* which decries the over-indulgent culture we live in and shows how to de-clutter our lives. The front cover asks, "Is your stuff weighing you down?" The article was directed toward those who "feel possessed by their possessions." If we are honest, we are likely to have felt this way, too.

Jesus made a point of this when telling the parable of the rich fool, found in Luke's gospel. In that story, Jesus tells of a man whose harvest was so big his storage wasn't enough. So he decides to build bigger barns into which he could store his grain and his goods so he could say to himself, "You have plenty of good things laid up for many years. Take life easy; eat, drink and be merry" (Luke 12:19). But he had no idea that his life was soon to end. Now what? Who will get what he has prepared for himself? Jesus gives this shocking conclusion: "This is how it will be for anyone who stores things for himself but is not rich toward God" (Luke 12:21).

Do we understand what Jesus is saying here? Some of us are building barns for ourselves rather than becoming rich toward God. Becoming rich toward God means storing up treasures in heaven, not treasures on earth.

It's hard to pray this prayer with sincerity when having so much. I sometimes find myself staring into my refrigerator full of good food and concluding that there's nothing to eat. Or what about when one of our kids says they don't have anything to wear when their closet is full of clothes?

We are all so rich compared to the world and there is no getting around the fact that, at varying degree, we are all hoarding wealth and resources for ourselves because we don't trust God to meet our needs. We hoard because we have this constant drive for more.

Recently I was having lunch at home and my wife was watching one of those real estate programs that show how the rich upper class live. The program featured a guy who had a huge house but an even bigger garage. It was an underground, 6,000 square foot facility that was accessed by a hydraulic lift big enough to drive a 40+ foot RV on it. When the lift came to ground level, there was artificial landscaping that matched the mountain exterior so it looked like the natural landscaping.

Inside the underground garage, the host walked around showing the owner's dozen cars, a huge RV, about 100 bikes and motorcycles and other collectibles. My wife and I were shaking our heads at the extravagance of this man's lifestyle, totally judging him for having so much wealth without even knowing how he is using his wealth in other ways.

Then something happened. I walked into my garage for something and noticed my wife's newish model Subaru AWD, my Harley Sportster, my kayak, my mountain bike and road bike and a bunch of tools and items that I take for granted. As I thought about this, I went back to my computer (that only the richest people on the planet own), pulled out my iPhone and set it next to my desk and sipped from a glass of clean water that I just got from the kitchen faucet and started back to work. As I began working, it hit me. "Compared to most people in the world, I'm as rich as the man on the TV program I had judged moments before. Am I as content as I should be?"

Jesus said, "It is easier for a camel to go through the eye of a needle than for a rich man to enter the kingdom of God" (Luke 18:25). Convicting, wouldn't you say, considering we are the richest country in the world. My late uncle Bill seemed to grasp this concept as he grew older. After he had become a widower, he methodically parceled out his resources to his children and various ministries he supported, keeping just enough money to not be a burden to his children whenever he stayed with them. The year before he passed, I had the chance to pay him a visit where he was staying with his son and daughter-in-law outside of Atlanta, Georgia.

We had a delightful dinner and enjoyed conversation about our shared extended family. After dessert, he wanted to show me where he was staying in their beautiful home. As we entered his room, I was amazed to see that all of his earthly possessions fit into a small carry on-sized suitcase. I asked where he kept everything else and with a smile he simply said, "I've given it all away. My goal is to leave this world with only the clothes on my back." Having blessed several ministries and his own family, he modeled what Jesus meant when describing someone who is rich toward God.

Let's get back to the subject at hand concerning our request for bread and how that relates to our serenity, or put another way, our contentment. In John's gospel we read more about the bread we are studying in The Lord's Prayer. Jesus has just finished providing bread to more than 5,000 and now the crowd is coming after him in hopes of receiving another free meal. Jesus tells the crowd, "I am the bread of life. He who comes to me will never go hungry, and he who believes in me will never be thirsty" (John 6:35).

Herein is the problem that many of us have when it comes to our consumerism tendencies and our lack of contentment. Somehow, we've not seen or experienced the loveliness and satisfaction that only Jesus can offer. The answer to a discontented life is to know Jesus more deeply. He is our contentment. He is our satisfaction. He's the One on whom we must fix our eyes because only then can we turn away from all our stuff and our incessant focus to build our kingdom so we can build His instead.

The blessing that occurs when we change our focus from building our kingdom to building His, is knowing that the things we need and are asking for will be given to us in the proper time. Here's how Jesus voiced this amazing promise: "But seek first His Kingdom and His righteousness, and all these things will be given to you as well" (Matthew 6:33).

OUR COMMUNITY

I've been saying since the beginning of this book that this prayer isn't an individualistic prayer. I don't mean we need to pray it publicly. You can pray this prayer alone but when you do, the very words cause you to consider the broader implication of those around you. The pronouns "us" and "our" in this petition alone serve to remind us of this. As I'm praying for my daily provision, I'm reminded that there are others who need the same things that I'm asking God to provide. I'm reminded as I pray for bread that there are millions around the world and thousands in our own backyard who don't have enough food to eat. As I pray this prayer, I'm moved to join in community efforts to help meet a need.

If Jesus used bread as an appropriate metaphor when asking God to meet our needs, it would make sense that meeting the physical needs of others ought to be our mission. William Booth, founder of the Salvation Army, was known for saying, "It's hard to preach the gospel to someone with an empty stomach." When we spiritualize this petition and discount the physical needs it represents, we tend to look at preaching the gospel as the only element of outreach worthy of our time or resources. But churches that realize that the gospel includes meeting people's physical needs see them as going hand-in-hand.

Sometimes it feels overwhelming. How can we put a dent in the hunger issue in our community and around the world? Or the need for clean drinking water for the millions who don't have immediate access to it? Or the need for medicines? There is need in every direction so it ought to be easy to do something. Where can you give "something" today? From every paycheck, where can you take a little of the extra you have for today and use it for someone who doesn't have enough? We can respond this way today because we trust God to provide for us tomorrow. Remember the Exodus manna? Enough for today, enough for tomorrow.

Did you know that the Greek word for "daily" used here is the only place in the New Testament where it is found? It's difficult to translate because there are no other references in Scripture to provide an interpretive guide. However, in secular writings where it is used, it connotes something you would find on a shopping list. In other words, it is the item you write down when you go to the store. In ancient times (and in many parts of our world today), shopping is a daily task. Many people simply go to the market for what is needed that day. That's because there's no refrigeration and no big box stores with millions of goods to choose from and buy in quantity. So it makes sense that when Jesus said we should ask God for our daily needs, He was likely referring to this daily trip to the market.

Many of us have been raised thinking that the saying, "God helps those who help themselves" comes from the Bible. It doesn't, but the Bible does say that we should help others. What if we viewed our help as the means by which God helps those who are truly in need? Some of us can give money, some can also give time, talents and even go to places where help is needed. Did you know you can volunteer in food banks and places that are trying to make a difference?

One of the things I love about the local church where I pastor is our CrossStreets ministry. CrossStreets began several years ago when one individual felt there were needs in our community that our church needed to address. Through prayer and with a small group of like-minded believers, Tom Green began taking ready-to-eat meals to places in our community where homeless people were living. Going out with this team on a Friday night is one of the most humbling and beautiful things one can do. Coming face to face with people who are struggling to live day-to-day and handing them items that help them is a beautiful expression of God's love. Since its inception, CrossStreets has fed tens of thousands of meals to hungry people and helped many to find their way back to a productive life. Through the years, our vision has grown to reach many people who need the gospel, but who are also hungry or needing some of the daily blessings most of us take for granted.

Now our church has hundreds of volunteers who serve in one of our venues that help people with their daily needs. It's exciting to see what happens when people give a little extra for the sake of those who don't have enough. That's what it's all about. When we pray the way Jesus taught us, we can't ask for our needs without thinking of the needs of others. When we think of them, God helps us give what we can so that their needs are met, too. What a great way to pray!

DISCUSSION QUESTIONS

1. Jesus' citation of "daily bread" was likely a reference to bread that came from heaven during Israel's wilderness wanderings. Take a moment to review this story found in Exodus 16:11-20 and respond to the following questions: A) Of all the things one might do with manna, what was the one thing no one could do? (see v.19); B) What are a couple of lessons that this story conveys to the one learning to pray, "Give us today our daily bread?"

2. What does the plural pronoun, "us" convey to the one who prays this petition? When have you experienced a change in your perspective about how much you own compared to so many people in the world? How long did your change in perspective last or has it been sustained? What are ways to sustain a changed perspective? If you have had extra bread for your daily needs, how have you shared it with others?

3. If "daily bread" represents our basic needs, what other kinds of things besides food do you suppose we should be asking God to provide for us? What did Jesus say to those who worry about things that God promises to take care of in our lives? (See Matthew 6:25-24)

4. On more than one occasion in the gospels, Jesus fed the multitudes starting with only a few loaves of bread (see John 6:1-15). How does this miracle relate to the

petition in The Lord's Prayer we are examining in this chapter? How does Jesus' follow up comments offer additional insight into the nature of this bread He makes available to us? See John 6:26-27; 35

5. As a group, draft a prayer-agenda that reflects the meaning of the fourth petition, *"Give us today our daily bread."* In other words, how would our prayers sound if we were trusting in God's provision to meet all of our needs?

6

EMBRACE HIS MERCY

"Forgive us our debts, as we also have forgiven our debtors..."
Matthew 6:12

I had just finished teaching our college mid-week meeting when Lisa walked up and asked if we could talk. We turned aside and with a very serious look on her face, she said, "I need to forgive the man who murdered my aunt." Until that moment, I hadn't known that Lisa had gone through something so traumatic. I asked her to fill me in. Holding back tears, she recounted the brutal and senseless murder which her aunt had fallen victim to a few years before. The murderer had been apprehended, tried in the court of law and was serving time on death row at San Quentin State Penitentiary.

My message that evening had obviously struck a chord in Lisa's heart. Unpacking the spiritual truth found in Jesus' parable of the unmerciful servant recorded in Matthew 18:21-35 had served as a conduit for Lisa's heart to act on what God had revealed in Scripture. In that parable, someone had been forgiven a great debt, but later punished another who had owed the newly forgiven one only a small debt. This placed the initial debtor in trouble with the one who had first forgiven him. Jesus used this story to reveal that forgiving others is the true litmus test of our understanding of God's forgiveness. If we don't forgive others for the comparatively small things people have done against us, how can we expect or believe that God will forgive our sins?

After all the paperwork had been filed and arrangements made, I went with Lisa to visit the man on death row and heard her speak loving forgiveness to a man who had brutally murdered someone in her own family. He was shocked and yet incredibly grateful that she made the effort to give him this priceless gift. I believe that after that meeting, neither of them were the same. Tony, the convicted murderer, got a glimpse of the power of being forgiven and Lisa understood even more deeply how forgiving someone brings transformation.

Thankfully, most of us don't wrestle with the need to forgive a murderer. But we frequently experience the need to forgive others for something they said or did to us, even if it isn't something terribly egregious. Our need to be forgiven and to forgive others is a common need for all of humanity. We are easily offended and often commit offenses. We say and do things that hurt others. We all carry relational wounds from the hurt that others have produced in our lives.

So it makes sense that our prayer life should include how we process the hurt that we've experienced or committed against others. Jesus knows this, of course, and specifically addresses this issue when teaching His disciples how to pray.

When we pray, Jesus said, we must include both our own need to be forgiven and our need to forgive others.

There are a total of six petitions in The Lord's Prayer and in this chapter we will examine the fifth, which reads, "Forgive us our debts, as we also have forgiven our debtors" (Matthew 6:12). Someone has aptly said that no written statement in the history of humanity has ever made more liars of us than this one. How true!

I shudder to think of the many times I've prayed this part of The Lord's Prayer, grateful for God's forgiveness for me, without recognizing that the prayer obligates me to forgive others, too. It's amazing how easy it is to call upon God's forgiveness and, at the same time, insinuate by this prayer that I've forgiven everyone around me when I really have not done so. For the sake of integrity, it would be better to omit this part of the prayer if I do not intend to place myself under the obligation it asserts. While an omission of that nature might help the sincerity of our prayers, it wouldn't improve our situation because the fact remains; we still need forgiveness ourselves. We can't omit it, instead, we must embrace it.

But this isn't easy to do. In our culture, there's a tendency to replace the concept of forgiveness with tolerance. For the past couple of decades, messages have emerged from our cultural powerhouses that tell us that the concept of sin is passé and handed down to us from irrelevant and ignorant sources. No one really needs forgiveness because there's really no such thing as being a sinner anymore. And to call people sinners is even worse! So in our culture, when people do things we don't like, or we do things they don't like, tolerance is what's needed, not forgiveness. Let's be clear. Tolerance doesn't come close to the true meaning of forgiveness.

Forgiveness is a great biblical concept and we must understand it thoroughly if we are going to offer it to others. The big takeaway from this petition found in The Lord's Prayer is simply this: We all need forgiveness and we all need to forgive others. That sounds pretty simple, doesn't it? It is, but just because something is simply understood doesn't mean it's easy. Let's look at four things that will help us not only understand this petition better, but also help with the heavy lifting when we pray this petition with sincere hearts.

A REMINDER

This petition reminds us that the core issue of the gospel is forgiveness. The gospel is essentially the good news about being forgiven by God. We are all sinners and in desperate need of God's forgiveness. It's important, however, to point out that each time we pray this prayer we are not asking God to save us again. Remember, Jesus is teaching His disciples, His followers and those who already belong to Him how to pray. He's not referring to their need for salvation when instructing them how to pray. This petition is intended to remind us of our conversion and that the entrance to salvation began by asking God for His forgiveness.

When we take this petition seriously, we can't help but be reminded of our conversion experience. The gospel only makes sense when we realize we are debtors to God and that we need forgiveness. I hear people sometimes articulate the gospel with no mention whatsoever of one's need for forgiveness. They may speak of "God's love" or that He helped save a marriage or that He blessed someone by giving them a better job. While these are all things that God may certainly provide for His children, they do not bring us to the core of its meaning.

The gospel, which in the Greek language means, "good news" (Gr., *eungelion*) declares that lost sinners like you and me are offered the free gift of forgiveness through faith in Jesus Christ. Jesus included this petition as a means for believers to have a regular reminder that our debt to God has been paid in full. The Bible claims that "all have sinned and fall short of the glory of God" (Romans 3:23) and, "The wages of sin is death, but the gift of God is eternal life in Christ Jesus our Lord" (Romans 6:23).

There are people who disagree with the assertion that they are sinners. They might justify their objection by comparing themselves to others by thinking "I'm not as bad as that guy." Or they may simply refuse to accept having a sin nature at all. People might also admit to what the Bible calls a sin nature with terms like, "shortcomings" or "mistakes" but the act of admitting we are sinners is not easy for some people.

King Solomon, who was known for his wisdom wrote "There is not a righteous man on earth who does what is right and never sins" (Ecclesiastes 7:20). In an earlier time of his life, Solomon asked, "Who can say, 'I have kept my heart pure; I am clean and without sin'"(Proverbs 20:9)? The answer, of course, is no one. The Apostle John probably had these two Scriptures in mind when he wrote "If we claim to be without sin, we deceive ourselves and the truth is not in us" (1 John 1:8).

But even with the knowledge of our sinfulness, the gospel offers sinners a righteousness apart from keeping the law of God, which is a righteousness that comes by faith (Romans 3:21-22; 5:1). When we believe in Christ's death and resurrection as both the payment for our sins and the power to live a new life, and begin following Jesus Christ, God no longer holds our sins against us. Hallelujah! We cry out with the Psalmist, "Blessed is he whose transgressions are forgiven, whose sins are covered. Blessed is the man whose sin the LORD does not count against him and in whose spirit is no deceit" (Psalms 32:1-2). Truly, the happiest and most contented people are those who are assured of God's forgiveness.

I point this out because I believe there may be someone reading this who has never received the gift of eternal life through repentance of sin and placing faith in Jesus Christ. If this describes you, consider how much God loves you and wants you to experience His forgiveness. He's offering it to you right now. Will you receive this gift?

OUR NEED FOR RENEWAL

This petition helps us realize our need for a daily spiritual renewal in our relationship with Jesus and others. We see this in the phrase, "Forgive us our debts..." If, as stated previously, we are confident this isn't a conversion prayer, it must be a cleansing prayer. Drawing closer to God and deepening our relationship with Him depends on admitting with regularity our need for His cleansing. That's what is in view here.

I like how the writer of Hebrews refers to this: "Therefore, since we have a great high priest who has ascended into heaven, Jesus the Son of God, let us hold firmly to the faith we profess. For we do not have a high priest who is unable to sympathize with our weaknesses, but we have one who has been tempted in every way, just as we are—yet was without sin. Let us then approach the throne of grace with confidence, so that we may receive mercy and find grace to help us in our time of need" (Hebrews 4:14-16). Did you notice here that the writer speaks about our need for grace to help us in our time of need? There's no doubt that our time of need might include cleansing from sins that nag and harass us.

Essentially, this petition is a fundamental reminder to all of us of our need for daily mercy. We are reminded by this petition that, while we have received new life through Christ, we are still in need of daily cleansing. That's what John had in mind when he wrote, "If we claim to be without sin, we deceive ourselves and the truth is not in us. If we confess our sins, he is faithful and just and will forgive us our sins and purify us from all unrighteousness" (1 John 1:8-9).

Even though our sins, past, present and future are completely forgiven at the moment of our conversion, there are things that unwittingly show up in our lives that remind us we are still sinners. We still snap at people with our words. We lust for things that are ungodly or harmful to us. We judge others due to personal pride or prejudice. We neglect serving and helping others in need. We hold on to our resources instead of sharing them. Every day, we fall short in varying degree in what God desires for us. This is our human condition even though we have become new creations through Jesus Christ.

The good news is that when we are saved, we possess the power to actually live in a different way and when we chose to obey Christ through the power of His Spirit, we do experience transformation. The Bible refers to this as our sanctification. But for as long as God gives us breath, we will struggle. We are free, but still at war in the spiritual realm.

On a technical note, some of our translations use different words for sin. Sometimes the word debt is used while at other times it is the word trespass. While there are slight nuances between the meaning of these words, essentially they serve to remind us there are various ways to say we've missed the mark that God wants in our relationship with Him or with others. To sin against God literally means to miss the mark of His perfection or holiness or to come up short. To trespass against Him is to go where we have no business going, such as when we become judgmental toward others when only God is the true judge. Or when we try to control our lives apart from God as our Sovereign leader. Or when we withhold from God what is rightfully His, such as our worship, money, time and especially our lives. Debts, trespasses and sins are all ways of saying the same basic thing — that we regularly fall short, cross the line and fail to give God what He deserves. We also do this in our relationships with others.

Have you agreed with God that something you have said, done or thought is not in alignment with His will for your life? If you do this regularly, it shows you understand what Jesus meant when teaching us to pray this way. The great news is that we can be assured that God has already pardoned all our sins (Ephesians 1:7) if we belong to Jesus Christ.

BELIEVE IT OR NOT

Praying this way means believing that God does forgive and, even more, that we can be assured of His forgiveness. Christ followers sometimes suffer from doubting God's forgiveness, leading to many harmful things. One of those things is an inner turmoil that immobilizes and keeps us from moving forward in our faith. I've met many believers who are still experiencing guilt over things they did in the past, even though they have confessed and repented of those things long ago. They are like prisoners in a cell with no doors or locks, choosing to stay bound by something that is no longer held against them. Is this you? Are you carrying the unnecessary burden of sins already forgiven? Whenever we sin, the first step is to confess our sin but what must follow is believing that God has forgiven us.

There are a few Scriptures that have always helped me when I find myself doubting God's forgiveness. Here are a few of my favorites:

"Though your sins are as scarlet, they shall be white as snow. Though they be red as crimson, they shall be as wool" (Isaiah 1:18).

"As far as the east is from the west; So far has He removed our transgressions from us" (Psalms 103:12).

"I, even I, am He who blots out your transgressions, for my own sake, and remembers your sins no more" (Isaiah 43:25).

Did you hear that? God forgives and remembers our sins no more. Some have said that God chooses to cast our sins even from his memory. I don't think that is possible since God is all-knowing. However, what it may point out is that God chooses no longer to hold these sins against us; He remembers them no more. What a miraculous blessing! Did you also notice that God forgives us more for His sake than ours? Forgiveness isn't so we can feel better about ourselves. God forgives us so that we can be in relationship with Him! That's why we should be eager to believe that God has forgiven us. It's not about us, it's about Him.

Some of us have a difficult time forgiving ourselves. Whenever this happens, we are playing the role of God, deciding if we deserve forgiveness or not. Our self-condemnation takes over and before we know it, we are convinced that we can't be forgiven — our sins are just beyond the reach of God's grace and mercy.

Karl Menninger of the Menninger Clinic once said that if he could convince the patients in his psychiatric hospitals that their sins really were forgiven, seventy-five percent of them could walk out the door of the hospital that very day. Many of us are creating huge obstacles to our emotional and psychological well-being simply because we refuse to believe that we are forgiven.

Perhaps for someone reading this, the light is finally coming on. You realize that God has completely forgiven you and you are free. Is there anything greater than this?

THE CATCH

Everything seems fine to us up to this point. Suddenly, however, as we look at the final part of this petition, we don't feel so comfortable. Asking God to forgive us? You bet. But what about being forgiven only insofar as we've forgiven those who have sinned against us? That doesn't feel so good. This is perhaps why St. Augustine of Hippo called this part of The Lord's Prayer, "The terrible petition."

What's interesting is that it is the only petition in The Lord's Prayer that includes a condition. You might even call it a catch. Here's what I believe Jesus has in mind here. He is wanting us to be accountable for how we treat others in relation to the way God treats us. He wants us to see that it makes no sense to ask God for forgiveness when we are not willing to pardon those who have sinned against us. The parable of the unmerciful servant illustrates this perfectly. The one who had been forgiven a great debt refused to forgive the one who owed him such a small debt, therefore, that man was severely punished. It was an untenable response considering the amount of grace he had been given.

It's amazing how blind we are to seeing this as a problem. How many times does something someone has said about us or done to us cause us to respond in anger and even hatred toward the person when we have committed far more serious offenses against God? We depend on God's forgiveness. We trust that His forgiveness is not only available, but also accessible to us every time we come to Him. But then we quickly forget all about this when we experience even the slightest grievance.

A married couple made an appointment with me to discuss a problem they were having. He was a businessman whose job required him increased travel each month. They were raising teenage kids and, apart from the occasional drama that having teenagers in the home can bring, their marriage had appeared to be going well. As she began to peel back the layers of her frustration, her husband confessed that he had been unfaithful to her on a recent business trip. I was shocked as he blurted out such terrible news. So was his wife. She became enraged, lashing out in anger over what he had done. She even began hitting him. He didn't even defend himself, knowing how wrong his actions had been and the damage he had caused. She finally calmed down enough to resume some discussion, though it wasn't long before they dismissed themselves and left my office. I worried that perhaps the marriage wouldn't survive. I thought of their kids. I thought of their Christian witness in the community. It was very sad.

A week later, they asked for another meeting with me. When they returned I could see that God was doing something special in their hearts. The husband had maintained a humble and contrite spirit and had not pressured her to forgive or take him back, though he made clear he had repented of his sin and wanted to somehow reconcile. God had softened her heart to the point of not only forgiving him, but also being willing to begin a process of reconciliation. Once it began, this process took months of counseling and honest sharing with each other but God brought them back together beautifully.

I remember asking her at one point in their process what had helped her most to forgive her husband for what he had done. She said something so simple, but profound, I've not forgotten it. She said, "Pastor Larry, I realized that no one could ever sin against me more than I've sinned against God. And if God has forgiven me, what right do I have to withhold forgiveness from my husband?" The realization of God's complete forgiveness opened the door for her to work on reconciliation and their marriage was eventually restored.

As we pray for our own sins to be forgiven, Jesus wants us to inventory our lives so that we can offer forgiveness to others. We become liars and insincere when we have no intention of forgiving others. This is why we need to pray the way Jesus taught us. We are forced to remember that the implied condition of our own forgiveness rests on our willingness to treat others the way God has treated us. Most times, this should happen within our hearts before any communication is needed toward an offending party. We should never go to anyone toward whom we have harbored unforgiveness (and they don't know it) and tell them, "I forgive you." They will likely ask, "For what?" and we will tell them how they hurt us (and this is what we want to do). We reason that if we have to forgive, we are at least going to let them know how much they have hurt us. This isn't what Jesus is talking about. Our forgiveness should not be a means to dredge up the offenses of others in order to take it out on them.

This is reiterated in verses 14-15 of Matthew 6, "For if you forgive men when they sin against you, your heavenly Father will also forgive you. But if you do not forgive men their sins, your Father will not forgive your sins." Yikes! Do we hear what Jesus is saying here? The proof that we understand and have received our own forgiveness will be that we forgive others. The Apostle Paul writes essentially the same thing to the Colossians: "Bear with each other and forgive whatever grievances you may have against one another. Forgive as the Lord forgave you" (Colossians 3:13).

Until or unless we forgive others from our hearts, we simply prove that we don't really have a clue about what God's forgiveness really means. We are to manifest forgiveness to others as the true badge of experiencing God's forgiveness. If forgiveness toward others is difficult even in trivial things, then it shows just how shallow we are in our understanding of God forgiving us.

Before finishing this chapter, I want to remind us once more that there is a difference between forgiving someone and reconciling with them. We are commanded to forgive, but reconciliation is a two-way street. It depends on the offending person's willingness to demonstrate honesty, or restitution for something damaged or stolen, and a period of time to pass so that trust can be reestablished and healing can occur. Remember, God loves reconciliation but the first step toward reconciliation is forgiveness, which isn't optional.

Is there a need to forgive someone who has sinned against you in some way? Jesus might as well be saying we should either get at it or quit praying this way. Might some of us be resisting the Holy Spirit if we pray this way without intending to demonstrate forgiveness ourselves? Is there someone who needs to hear you say, "I forgive you?" Does someone owe you a debt you are willing to cancel? Is there anyone toward whom you have harbored ill feelings due to words they have said to you, or about you to someone else? Are you willing to forgive them and waste no time letting them know your heart is no longer embittered against them? Fredrick Buechner put it this way, "To forgive someone is to say one way or another, 'You have done something unspeakable, and by all rights I should call it quits between us. However, although I make no guarantees that I will be able to forget what you've done and though we may both carry the scars for life, I refuse to let it stand between us. I still want you to be my friend" (Quoted in "The Lord's Prayer for Today" by William Carl.)

Maybe we need to go to someone in person to ask for forgiveness. If going to them in person isn't possible, then we could send a letter or even an email. Maybe the same can be done for someone we need to forgive. If we take the prayer Jesus taught seriously, then we will respond and become agents of transformation in our world.

DISCUSSION QUESTIONS

1. What is the biggest financial debt you have ever been forgiven? What did it feel like to have the debt cancelled?

2. Why is it generally easier to ask for God's forgiveness than to forgive those who have wronged or sinned against us? Why are we more keenly aware of the wrongs and sins others have committed against us, than those wrongs and sins we've committed against others?

3. If all of our sins (past, present and future) are forgiven through a relationship with Jesus Christ (Ephesians 1:7; Colossian 1:14), why did Jesus teach us to pray, *"Forgive us our debts...?*

4. Carefully read through the parable recorded in Matthew 18:21-35 (try to read this in an NIV translation) and answer the following questions: A) Why did Jesus tell this story? What is it meant to illustrate? B) What is the point of irony in the story that Jesus wants Peter (and us) to understand? C) How does v.35 relate to the section in The Lord's Prayer we are examining?

5. Why is it sometimes difficult for Christ-followers to admit their sin and seek forgiveness from God? What does the Bible say about the person who denies their sin? (See 1 John 1:8-9). How should we deal with our sin according to 1 John 1:9?

6. To what degree do you feel Christ followers truly understand and embrace God's forgiveness in their lives?

Has this ever been a struggle for you? If so, what did you do about it?

7. As a group, draft a prayer-agenda that reflects the meaning of the fifth petition, *"Forgive us our debts, as we forgive our debtors."* In other words, how would our prayers sound if we were embracing God's mercy in our own lives and extending it to others?

7

RELY ON HIS PROTECTION

"Lead us not into temptation, but deliver us from the evil one."
Matthew 6:13

I like the prayer I once heard: "Lord, so far today, I've done alright. I haven't gossiped or lost my temper. I haven't fallen to temptation. I haven't been greedy, grumpy, nasty, selfish or overindulgent. I'm thankful for this. But in a few minutes, God, I'm going to get out of bed and from then on, I'm going to need a lot more help. Amen." As humorous as that prayer may sound, it does bear an important truth from the moment we arise to start our day, we need God's guidance and protection.

We are engaged in a spiritual battle that wages war on our souls every day. If it isn't the pull of our flesh toward things that can harm us or dishonor God, it's the incessant attack of our enemy, the devil, who prowls around like a roaring lion looking for someone to devour (1 Peter 5:8). Whether we realize this or not, it's the truth. To ignore or neglect this truth is to do so at our own peril.

Scripture declares, "...our struggle is not against flesh and blood, but against the rulers, against the authorities, against the powers of this dark world and against the spiritual forces of evil in the heavenly realms" (Ephesians

6:12). We're tempted to view those with whom we are in conflict as our enemies when in reality, there are forces at work all around us that are far more malevolent. For this reason, the Apostle Paul admonishes that we put on the full armor of God, so that when the day of evil comes, we may be able to stand our ground" (Ephesians 6:13).

In this passage which offers such amazing insight about our spiritual battles, the actual pieces of armor are identified. There's the belt of truth, the breastplate of righteousness and proper shoes fitted for taking our stand for the gospel. There's also the shield of faith, the helmet of salvation and the sword of the Spirit. All these pieces point to how we are to spiritually prepare and arm ourselves for battle. At the end of this critical list of personal armor Paul adds, "And pray in the Spirit on all occasions with all kinds of prayers and requests. With this in mind, be alert and always keep on praying for all the saints" (Ephesians 6:18). For the Apostle Paul and for all of us, prayer holds everything together.

It's clear that spiritual warfare and our need for protection was in the heart of Jesus when He taught His disciples how to pray. He said when we pray, we should say, "And lead us not into temptation, but deliver us from the evil one" (Matthew 6:13). After everything we've learned so far about this prayer and what it means, we turn now to this final petition which shows us the importance Jesus Himself puts on

His followers for being prepared to deal with forces that would seek to undo them.

In this final petition, we immediately see two very important realities. The first deals with temptation and the second with our adversary, the devil. The use of the conjunction "but" between these two realities shows how they go together. In this petition, we are asking God not to lead us into temptation but rather, deliver us from our adversary.

I should point out here that the word translated "temptation" in Matthew 6:13 comes from the Greek word, *"peirasmos."* This word is used 21 times in the New Testament and can also be translated "trials" or "testing." Whenever this word shows up in a text, New Testament translators choose the word which best fits the context of the passage. In most cases it is translated into our English word "temptation." Let's begin by reviewing some important truths about temptation. Perhaps this will help us understand why when we pray, we should petition God to not lead us into temptation.

Truth #1: TEMPTATION DOESN'T COME FROM GOD

We begin by underscoring that God never tempts anyone. The Apostle James writes: "When tempted, no one should say, 'God is tempting me.' For God cannot be tempted by evil, nor does he tempt anyone; but each one is tempted when, by his own evil desire, he is dragged away and enticed. Then, after desire has conceived, it gives birth to sin; and sin, when it is full-grown, gives birth to death" (James 1:13-15). According to this text, we can be assured that, while God may indeed send trials our way, He never sends temptation. He also may test us but he never tempts us. That's why in James' epistle we read, "Consider it pure joy, whenever you face trials of many kinds…" (James 1:2).

The word "trials" is translated from the same Greek word that is also found in James 1:13 where it is translated, "temptation." Again, the contexts help us see why they are different. If James wrote, "When tested, no one should say, 'God is testing me,'" we would discover an obvious contradiction in the Bible. That's because throughout Scripture we learn that God may send trials and tests to His people for the purpose of seeing what's in their hearts and as a means for their spiritual growth. According to the Apostle James, God uses trials, not temptation, to develop endurance in our lives.

Here's another thing. While it is certainly true that temptation can come from Satan himself, most often its origin is within ourselves. Note the condemning reality: "…but each is tempted when, by his own evil desire, he is dragged away and enticed…" (James 1:14). If we struggle with maintaining a healthy diet because we have a sweet tooth, we have no one to blame but ourselves if we go on a binge at Krispy Kreme Donuts. Succumbing to the temptations that arise within our own hearts can be far more serious than eating too many donuts, but you get the point. We don't need to worry too much about an external force taking us down. There's plenty of inappropriate promptings that come from within.

Truth #2: TEMPTATION ISN'T SIN

Sometimes we confuse temptation with sin. There's no sin inherent in temptation unless we do what we are tempted to do. Even Jesus experienced temptation and if He experienced it, we can count on experiencing it, too. It's a reality in all our lives.

There's something so encouraging whenever we find ourselves being tempted: "...we do not have a high priest who is unable to sympathize with our weaknesses, but we have one who has been tempted in every way, just as we are—yet was without sin. Let us then approach the throne of grace with confidence, so that we may receive mercy and find grace to help us in our time of need" (Hebrews 4:15-16). It amazes me to realize that Jesus was tempted as we are, yet He was without sin! The pull of temptation abates temporarily when we give in to its urging, but this wasn't true for Jesus. Throughout His earthly ministry, He battled temptation and was victorious over it every time! This is why the writer of Hebrews encourages his reader to come before God with an attitude of confidence when in a time of need.

If you find yourself facing a lot of temptation, perhaps you're not praying enough ahead of time for God to keep you from it. Because our hearts are deceptive and we often flirt with a temptation before we ever fall into it, we need to be prayerfully wary of our weaknesses. Prayer engages our hearts with the reminder that we're likely to get into trouble if we keep going down a certain path. But if we don't sincerely ask God to mediate our choices and exposure to things we struggle with, we have a much higher probability of failing. This is what's behind the petition for God not to lead us into temptation. We ask for this because we often lead ourselves into temptation and we need divine assistance to avoid it.

I'm convinced that prayerlessness is often one of the biggest reasons people continue to fall into a certain sin. When you pray, you can depend on your great High Priest, Jesus Christ, who will give you the mercy and grace you need. Remember, the temptation really isn't the problem. Being tempted isn't a sin. It's what happens after the temptation that determines whether or not sin has been committed.

Truth #3: GOD NEVER ALLOWS US TO BE TEMPTED BEYOND WHAT WE ARE ABLE TO BEAR

We've already said that temptation never comes directly from God but we have to concede the point that God allows us to be tempted. Being a follower of Christ doesn't insulate us from any and all temptations. We are assured from Scripture that whenever temptation does come to our door, it doesn't have the power to overcome our own will. I've met people (and thought this way myself at times) who say they are powerless to deny a certain temptation, as if it imposes its own will over them. This is a lie that Satan uses to make us feel defeated before we even start resisting it. God knows the level of our resistance to temptation and He promises to not allow us to be tempted at a level that we cannot resist.

The Apostle Paul clarifies this to the Corinthians when he writes: "No temptation has seized you except what is common to man. And God is faithful; He will not let you be tempted beyond what you can bear. But when you are temped, He will provide a way out so that you can stand up under it" (1 Corinthians 10:13). This is one of God's greatest promises to us as His children. He superintends every temptation that comes to us according to what He knows we can handle. Even more, He promises a way of escape when the temptation is bearing down on us.

Years ago, some friends and I had the chance to board a flight simulator at Travis Air Force Base. It was a training tool for pilots who were learning to fly C-5A's, which are the Air Force's jumbo cargo jets. The flight instructor gave us a short orientation showing how realistic the "flying" experience was to students. Then he told us it was our turn to take the controls. We all traded off sitting in various seats; pilot, co-pilot, navigator and felt what it's like to be at the controls of such a magnificent aircraft. With the instructor's help, we were able to take off and work our way up to a safe cruising speed at the normal range of altitude. We all started feeling pretty good about our skills until he would say something like, "Okay, we're going to turn off engines #2 and #3 and see what happens." Or, "You have a fire in the cargo area that is spreading rapidly! You must take emergency measures now!" The simulator was so realistic, our emergency responses led us into one disastrous move after another, each time ending up with buzzers going off and computers shouting, "Prepare for impact!" Needless to say, we all realized quickly that if our lives depended on getting the aircraft safely down, we didn't stand a chance.

Student pilots are trained to deal with emergency issues that arise in flight and good instructors don't introduce crisis scenarios beyond a student's preparation. This is even more true of the way God works in our lives. Sure, temptations arise, but according to Paul's words in 1 Corinthians, we can be assured that God doesn't ever allow a scenario that we cannot handle. He keenly knows exactly where a situation surpasses our ability to resist and He promises to never let this happen. If we crash and burn, it isn't because God hasn't done His part. It's simply because we chose to battle the temptation on our own, apart from God's limitless resources.

While it's encouraging to know that God has promised us a way out of temptation, it's also very convicting knowing that if we have failed a test, we didn't need to. God is faithful and keeps all his promises (Psalms 145:13).

John Ortberg, in his book on The Lord's Prayer, uses an illustration about a bug zapper to remind his readers of the importance of not going past boundaries meant to keep us safe and in God's will. When we look around our culture, when we read the news or when we talk to our friends, do we ever hear the tell-tale "zap" that means someone has come too close to the fire? The book of Proverbs sheds light on this very thing when Solomon asks, "Can a man scoop fire into his lap without his clothes being burned? Can a man walk on hot coals without his feet being scorched? So is he who sleeps with another man's wife; no one who touches her will go unpunished" (Proverbs 6:27-29).

This gets to the core of praying that God would not lead us into temptation. He's simply pointing out that we are often drawn to places and situations that pose some level of temptation so we ask God not to let us go to them. Where are those places for you? Some of us have little secret areas where we like to play the game of how close can we get and not succumb? Do we pray this way? God doesn't want us to experience the proverbial bug-zapper when we go too far. Admitting to God where we are weak can break spiritual strongholds in our lives. We prove how strong we are not by how we cope with being tempted, but by seeing how far we can stay away from the temptation that could undo us.

Truth #4: WE HAVE THE GREATEST HELP POSSIBLE WHENEVER WE FIND OURSELVES IN TEMPTATION

Whenever we feel we might be on the verge of falling to temptation, we have the best available resource possible. That resource of course is the Lord Jesus Christ and our help is only a prayer away. Hebrews 2:18 tells us: "Because He Himself suffered when he was tempted, He is able to help those who are being tempted" (Hebrews 2:18). This is why I love Jesus. He is able to help me when I'm tempted and He will help you, too. Our Savior is ready to come to our aid when we realize we are getting in over our head. Many of us simply wait too long before we ask Him for help. We need to remember that it's easier to stay out of trouble than to get out of trouble. That's the point of this petition.

Are you asking daily not to be led into temptation? Are you looking for ways of escape when the temptation comes knocking? As someone once said, "Temptation will come knocking but you don't have to open the door."

THE EVIL ONE

Now that we have a little more understanding about what the first part of the petition means, let's look at the second part. What is behind the phrase, "...but deliver us from the evil one?" Essentially, this is about the importance of being mindful of Satan, our greatest enemy. There's a humorous story that William Carl tells about a woman who

150

would come out on her front porch each day, raise her hands and say out loud, "Praise the Lord!" An atheist moved in next door to her and soon became annoyed by this woman's incessant praises to God. He would sometimes yell back from his porch, "There is no God!" One day, the woman was in trouble and she went out on the porch and called, "O Lord! Help me. I have no more money this month and I am hungry and need food." The next morning, when she came outside there on her porch were several bags of groceries, enough for a week. She cried out loud, "Praise the Lord, you have saved my life!" The atheist stepped out from behind the bushes and said, "You fool, God didn't answer your prayers. I bought you those groceries and put them there myself!" The woman looked to heaven and said, "Praise the Lord! You sent me groceries and you got the devil to pay for and deliver them!"

If we depend on God and make Him the object of our praise, we might be surprised how He will answer our prayers in the midst of our spiritual battles. As we pray in alignment with this phrase, here are some simple facts we should keep in mind about the evil one.

FACT #1: HE IS REAL

Satan is not a fairy tale and he doesn't wear a red flannel suit nor does he carry a pitchfork. At one time, he was God's highest ranking angel, a created being who turned away from Almighty God and incited a rebellion in heaven before

God stripped him of his position. One of the most dangerous places a believer can find himself is trivializing or minimizing the reality of Satan's existence.

His existence is clearly revealed throughout Scripture. He was there in the garden tempting Adam and Eve to distrust and disobey God. His successful strategy put into motion the curse that has swept over all of humanity. God offers the only solution through the death and resurrection of Jesus Christ. Satan is active in our world today and will continue to be until God finally puts an end to his influence and, eventually, his existence.

The Apostle John refers to him in the Book of Revelation as, "The great dragon—that ancient serpent called the devil, or Satan who leads the whole world astray" (Revelation 12:9). The writers of Scripture make clear that he's no made-up being but believers today are sometimes duped into thinking he's not for real.

FACT #2: HE'S YOUR ONE TRUE ENEMY

Though defeated by Jesus at the Cross (1 John 3:8), Satan would destroy you if he could. The spiritual trials of our lives and the friction we feel in the world are not a result of mere human injustices and problems between people. Paul reminds the Ephesians that "our struggle isn't against flesh and blood..." He'd love you to think that your real problem is with your husband or wife, your son or daughter, your mom or your dad, a neighbor, a coworker or some random stranger. In reality, Satan is our REAL problem. Martin Luther's great hymn, *"A Mighty Fortress Is our God"* speaks of him this way: "A mighty fortress is our God—a bulwark never failing. Our helper He, amid the flood of mortal ills prevailing...For still our ancient foe, Doth seek to work us woe; His craft and power are great—and armed with cruel hate—On earth is not his equal..." He's real and he's our one true enemy.

Jesus calls him the thief who comes to steal, kill and destroy (John 10:10). This is an accurate description of our enemy, a master thief who knows how to steal what's precious from our lives. Spiritual death and destruction follow in the wake of his malicious systems and strategies.

FACT #3: HE IS A LIAR AND USES DECEPTION AS HIS PRIMARY WEAPON

Everything Satan says is a lie. How do you know when he's lying? Whenever he speaks. He is incapable of telling the truth unless the truth in some way serves his purpose or he is seeking to manipulate his victim. When he confronts Jesus in the wilderness to tempt him, he quotes truth but out of context. Even when he tells the truth, he's in some way lying about it. This is his method. He's the father of lies (John 8:44). The problem with his lies is that often they can sound plausible and even compelling.

Believers get into trouble quickly when they buy into the devil's lies. Because our hearts are deceitful (Jeremiah 17:9) we are vulnerable to confusing truth with error. I'm ashamed of the many times I've pursued something thinking it was within the bounds of God's plan for me, only to realize later I'd bought into one of Satan's lies. If you are honest, you will likely see this in your life, too.

Of course, it's easier to see this in the lives of others than in our own. One of our believing friends may decide to leave her spouse because she feels the need to be with someone who is more compatible with her interests. When you confront this decision, she assures you that she feels this is God's will for her life. A question we should always ask ourselves whenever we sense something being God's will is this: Does God's Word have anything to say about it? I've heard people justify adultery, pornography, addictions, greed and a host of things clearly labeled as sin in Scripture. This is because Satan is a liar, a master deceiver.

FACT #4: HE CANNOT PENETRATE OUR SPIRITUAL ARMOR

Of the many things we might say are facts about our enemy, this is one for which we can be thankful. If we are wearing the armor of God, as revealed to us in Ephesians 6:10-18, our prayers of protection will be honored by God. I like what my Greek professor used to say, "...if you studied for the exam, your prayers will help, but if you didn't study, don't expect prayer to do that much for you." I've never forgotten that statement and I found his logic to be true. The exams that God helped me with were the ones I had studied for the most. So God says, "…wear the armor. If you do, your prayers of protection will help." Are you wearing your spiritual armor? If you are, prayer really helps; if not, prayer isn't as impactful.

The armor that the Apostle Paul identifies in Ephesians isn't a wardrobe of tangible items, much like a soldier would keep in his footlocker. Nevertheless, they are just as real. In the same way that our struggle isn't against flesh and blood, but with powers in the spiritual realm, so our armor describes the spiritual protection available to every believer.

The belt of truth represents the believer's sincerity in walking with Christ. When we refuse to allow hypocrisy to settle into an area of our Christian walk, we are wearing the belt of truth.

The breastplate of righteousness represents our obedience to the moral law of God. While believers receive an imputed righteousness by faith alone, here the focus is on how our practical obedience protects us from the enemy's firepower. Nothing like subtle compromise or outright disobedience to make us vulnerable to the enemy's attack.

Feet fitted with the readiness that comes from the gospel of peace may be referring to our settled belief in the gospel and our passion to declare it boldly wherever we are. Remember, the armor is to help us take our stand against the enemy, and to do so requires a firm and unwavering belief in the power and effectiveness of the gospel.

The shield of faith represents one's belief in God's truth. To believe what God has said is an extremely powerful protection against the enemy's lies. His flaming arrows are an attempt to discount everything God has said to His people. Without the shield in place, we are extremely vulnerable to taking vicious hits from the enemy.

The helmet of salvation represents one's assurance of salvation. The enemy loves it when we doubt the work of God in bringing us spiritual life and the only way to defend ourselves from this doubt is to be secure in our position.

The sword of the Spirit, which Paul says is the word of God, needs no explanation. Knowing God's Word and hiding it in our hearts is our greatest defense of all. This piece of armor is the only one used both defensively and offensively. It's both a lethal weapon and a formidable defense against the enemy's tactics.

It's also interesting that, included in this amazing list of armor, is prayer. We'll take a closer look at that in the final chapter.

In conclusion, our prayers should reflect what we've learned here about temptation and our enemy. If they do, we'll overcome the temptations we face and experience all the protection we need.

DISCUSSION QUESTIONS

1. If the Bible tells us that God doesn't tempt people, why would Jesus tell us to pray "not to be led into temptation?" What is the point Jesus is getting at here?

2. Whenever we do experience temptation, what are some things, according to 1 Corinthians 10:13, that we can be absolutely sure of?

3. All of us have areas in our lives that present potential pitfalls but they are no different from those of others. In knowing this, what is at the core of the petition, "Lead us not into temptation?" Identify areas that easily ensnare people.

4. Think about this statement and talk about it in your group: *"It's easier to stay out of trouble than to get out of trouble."* Have you ever placed yourself in an environment where a temptation got you into trouble? What did you learn?

5. What are believers instructed to do in order to take their stand against the devil's schemes? (See Ephesians 6:10-18)

6. As a group, draft a prayer-agenda that reflects the meaning of the sixth petition, *"And lead us not into temptation, but deliver us from the evil one."* In other words, how would our prayers sound if we were avoiding areas where we might fall to temptation and also embracing God's protection when under attack?

8

PRAYER FOR EVERY SEASON

"...and pray in the spirit on all occasions..."
Ephesians 6:18a

Knowing how to pray is an essential discipline for our lives and this book was written in order to help the reader understand how it is done. But learning how to pray as Jesus taught us is just the beginning of an active and productive prayer life. The study of prayer is virtually inexhaustible. After a life-long journey of prayer, there is still much to learn. It is my hope that this book will not only help get our prayer journey started, but also keep it going.

When examining my own prayer journey through five decades of walking with Jesus, I've learned the importance of not only knowing how to pray, but when to pray. The Bible has much to say about when prayer should be our first and sometimes only response to the circumstances we face.

In this final chapter, I'd like to offer some practical insights for when prayer should be viewed as the best option in the midst of our circumstances. In his letter to the Ephesians, the great Apostle Paul emphasized this when writing: "And pray in the Spirit on all occasions with all kinds of prayers and requests. With this in mind, be alert and always keep on praying for all the saints" (Ephesians 6:18).

You don't need to be a Bible scholar to understand Paul's point. He's reminding his reader to pray at all times about everything. This may seem impossible at first, but God never commands us to do anything that He hasn't already given us the capacity to do. Whatever He commands, He enables.

Praying all the time about everything is put even more succinctly in 1 Thessalonians 5:17 where Paul writes, "…pray continually" or, as another translation has it, "…pray without ceasing." Really? Is this even possible? How can we go through an entire day doing nothing else but praying about everything in our lives? Don't we have to work? Don't we have to communicate with loved ones? What does this really mean?

God isn't calling us into a monastic life where we confine ourselves to only pray and do nothing else. If this were true, He wouldn't have instructed us how to do our work (Colossians 3:23), or love our wives (Ephesians 5:25) or respect our husbands (Ephesians 5:33). He wouldn't have taught us that we should be generous with our resources and give to the poor (Proverbs 28:27) or that we should eagerly serve God's people using the spiritual gifts God's Spirit has given us (1 Peter 4:10). Of course we must live our lives, which involves giving our attention to many things. But what God does call us to do is to breathe prayer into every situation, opportunity, pursuit, interest and relationship in our lives. It is a prayer posture that God is calling us to assume so that whatever we do, or wherever we are, we are purposefully connecting with God through prayer.

If we are honest, we must admit that often, prayer is the last thing we do in many of life's situations. It's like we are hardwired to not trust the One who alone has the answer or resources we need. I've heard people even say (and I've said it myself), "Well, I guess the only thing we can do now is pray." Actually, prayer is needed at the start of the matter and should continue while going through it, even when eventually coming out on the other side of the situation. Do you believe this? Perhaps you do but you may wonder how to make it practical in your life. Good, because that's what this closing chapter is all about.

I've discovered there are many seasons and situations in life where God wants us to be especially mindful of seeing prayer as a means of drawing closer to Him. I offer just three of these seasons, hoping they will whet your appetite to go after prayer no matter in what season or situation you may find yourself. These seasons correspond to three amazing New Testament texts on the matter of prayer.

A SEASON OF WORRY

All of us have things about which we are tempted to worry. We worry about our health. We worry about our kids. We worry about our job. We worry about money, friendships and our future; we can worry about anything and everything.

What are you tempted to worry about? If you're like me, on any given day there are a number of things to worry about.

Worry is a choice. It's also a sin. To worry is to assume that it's our job to stay in control of everything going on around us, or perhaps in us. To worry is to take the place of God. We like to be the ones calling all the shots but when things don't go in the direction we want them to go, or we feel something is spinning out of control, worry takes over. We've all been there. Sleeplessness, depression, anxiety and even physical illness can often be traced to things we are worried about.

Seasons that are likely to set off worry in our lives are perfect times to pray. In fact, God wants us to view prayer as the proper antidote for worry. That's what the Apostle Paul wrote about in the book of Philippians: "Do not be anxious about anything, but in everything, by prayer and petition, with thanksgiving, present your requests to God" (Philippians 4:6). Paul is saying that the best thing we can do when we find ourselves tempted to worry is simply to pray about it.

A little textual note is important here. Notice Paul writes, "...prayer and petition, with thanksgiving..." The word we translate, "prayer" (Gr. *proseuche*) is a word that describes the attitude in which we come to God. It is a word that describes worship and adoration of God. Here's something worth thinking about. From what we read in Philippians 4:6, it's possible to turn worry into worship. How? By bringing our anxious thoughts to God and trusting Him for whatever He wants to do in the situation or season that is tempting us to worry. I know this is easier said than done — boy do I know!

Worry is a sin that has dogged me all my life. My mom even gave me the nickname, "worry-wart" as a young child. It seemed that I worried about lots of things and people around me could see it plain as day. Thankfully, God has redeemed and transformed me, but my natural default is to worry about things. I continue to learn the importance of choosing an attitude of trust which promotes an active and vibrant prayer life.

When your child goes off to college and moves into the dorm you must turn your worry into worship through prayer. When your marriage shows signs of erosion and you are tempted to think the worst, turn your worry into worship through prayer. When your boss tells you that the company needs to lay off employees, turn your worry into worship through prayer. When your doctor tells you she needs a follow up appointment to discuss your tests, turn your worry into worship through prayer! Every situation is an opportunity to worship God through prayer.

Moving from the more general word for prayer, Paul tells his readers to bring their "petition..." Petitions are specific requests that we articulate to God as we worship him in prayer. You can trust God for your daughter moving off to college, but you can specifically ask God to bring godly friendships into her life. You can ask God to give her wisdom to make good choices. You can ask God to protect her from the devil's schemes. Prayer must not only be a posture of worshipful trust, but also a means to articulate specific things that we need to God. God loves to hear the specifics, not because He needs to be better informed, but because He wants to answer our prayers specifically.

Notice also from the Philippian passage that, along with our worshipful posture and our specific requests, God tells us to be grateful, "...with thanksgiving, present your requests to God" (Philippians 4:6). Why is gratitude important? Because when we thank God in advance for what we are asking Him to do, it shows we are trusting Him for the outcome. Gratitude is our way of saying to God, "You are in control and I trust You to take care of this in the way that brings most honor and glory to You."

What happens when we pray this way in seasons when we are tempted to worry? The text tells us, "...and the peace of God, which transcends all understanding, will guard your hearts and your minds in Christ Jesus" (Philippians 4:7). When we pray in seasons of worry, our worry subsides as we offer our prayers to God, allowing His peace to guard our mental and emotional well-being.

I've experienced this enough times to trust God's promises. In some of the most difficult experiences I've faced in my family or ministry, God's peace has been there for me whenever I've turned to Him in worshipful, specific and grateful prayer. Recently I was feeling tempted to worry about the spiritual condition of one of my adult children. Sensing this, my friend Helena, a dear sister in Christ, shared a quote from Sharon Lagueux which she believed might help: "When your arms can't reach people who are close to your heart, you can always hug them with your prayers." This spoke deeply to me.

It was the reminder I needed. Turning to God in that moment to share my concerns immediately ushered in that peace that God promised. I'm grateful for friends who point me to the power of prayer, especially when I'm tempted to worry.

Maybe you are worrying about something right now. Will you accept God's instruction and turn your worry into a moment of worship by trusting God while bringing your specific requests to Him? Will you offer your gratitude as a deposit of trusting God that the outcome of the matter will be for your good and His glory? Take a few moments before moving on from here, to bring your request to God and allow His peace to guard your heart and mind for what is ahead.

A SEASON OF WEAKNESS

If there is something easily learned about prayer it's realizing we don't always know exactly what to say when we approach God. There are seasons and situations we encounter that create a struggle to know the right words to offer to God. I've often found myself feeling inept while searching for the right words to say in prayer. When I feel this way, prayer is often moved to the back burner. Maybe you've found yourself in situations or seasons in life where prayer has virtually been absent, even amidst very challenging times.

The curious absence of prayer in difficult times may stem from being unsure about what to say to God. If you have experienced this, I want to encourage you with Romans 8:26-27: "In the same way, the Spirit helps us in our weakness. We do not know what we ought to pray for, but the Spirit Himself intercedes for us with groans that words cannot express. And He who searches our hearts knows the mind of the Spirit, because the Spirit intercedes for the saints in accordance with God's will."

This "weakness" Paul speaks about in Romans 8, through which the Spirit desires to help us, is explained as not knowing the things for which we should pray. It's when we feel weak in our prayers we need to rely on the Spirit's intercession on our behalf. We might stumble our way through a prayer not really knowing what to ask for, but the Spirit of God knows exactly what we need and conveys these things to our loving and gracious heavenly Father "…in accordance with God's will" (Romans 8:27). It's reassuring to depend on the Spirit to help us in our weakness even when we don't know the things for which we should pray.

Sometimes I observe how new believers shy away from praying in a public setting simply because they haven't had much experience praying this way. When I have the opportunity, I encourage them to not worry about their words, reminding them of Romans 8. I tell them, "The Spirit will do all the translating so that you can be assured God will hear your prayer and answer you according to His perfect will." Sometimes they take my advice and decide to give it a shot. Prayers that newer believers pray are often the most blunt and unpolished prayers one might ever hear. Their simplicity and honesty may even bring a smile or a chuckle to listeners. I sometimes wonder who takes more pleasure in hearing them; the Spirit who is translating, or the Father who searches our hearts as He listens. What matters is that our prayers are heard and formed by the Spirit in a way that conforms to God's will.

When I was in high school, I remember praying that God would allow me to have my own car. I had very specific ideas that I felt God should know about in discussing the car He would one day provide for me. It would have a large block engine with a muffler that made it sound "mean" as it roared past the school, making all my friends jealous that my car was so amazing. My prayers were very sincere but unfortunately not very mature. I obviously didn't know what I ought to pray for. But no worries! The Spirit was interceding according to the will of God for my life. My first car, the answer to my prayers, was a 1959 VW Beetle. It was my dad's commuter car and after it had about a hundred thousand original miles, he felt God would have him give it to me. God answered my prayer even though it wasn't really what I had been asking for every day for nearly a year. But God the Spirit knew exactly what I needed and the Father was pleased to give it to me.

The same could be said of my youthful prayers for meeting and eventually marrying the right woman. I was convinced I had met her in my freshman year of high school. She was a beautiful blonde with brown eyes so large that my friend and I affectionately referred to her privately between us as, "Cow-eyes." (We never let her know this!) She was "the one" and I knew it. So I just kept asking God to make her like me so that someday we could settle down and have lots of baby calves together.

The trouble was that I didn't really know what to pray for. The Spirit kept right on speaking to the Father about my requests even though "Cow-eyes" never did show any interest in me. As I grew, the few other girls who got my attention — even some of them who allowed me to date them — didn't seem to work out. I'm sure it had nothing to do with my quirkiness or goofy ways. However, the Spirit knew who I needed and one day, in God's perfect timing, He opened her eyes to see me and my eyes to see her, and we've made a beautiful life together for 35 years, and we're just getting started! God was so gracious to bring such a beautiful and

Christ-loving woman into my life and to give both of us the wisdom to make this commitment together. Don't get me wrong, it hasn't been easy all the time. Just ask my wife! She puts up with a lot.

Knowing that the Spirit translates our prayers to the Father according to His will is one of the most amazing realities we can celebrate as followers of Christ. No matter what we are going through, no matter how confusing things might be, trust that as we pray, the Spirit is at work translating our heart's desire into the perfect will of God. This reality should keep us steadfast in prayer.

Perhaps you are holding back in your prayers for something right now because you simply don't know how to pray. You are unsure of what God's will is. You feel conflicted or in some way hindered to just let the words flow. Might I suggest you throw caution to the wind and just let God hear your heart? You can be assured that the Spirit will translate and the Father will see what's in your heart and God will move in a way that is aligned with His will for you. Prayer isn't a magic wand that gets us what we want. It allows God to shape our lives and move us to where He is wanting us to go. That's why prayer also takes time. It's rarely pray now and have an answer minutes after you say "amen."

A SEASON OF GOOD WORKS

Thoughtful believers realize that God is on display in their lives everywhere they go. Jesus taught his disciples, "You are the light of the world. Let your light shine before men, that they may see your good deeds and praise your Father in heaven" (Matthew 5:14,16). While our works don't save us, God uses our good works done with right motives to touch the hearts of an unbelieving world.

This is where prayer again plays an important role in our lives. In John 14, Philip, one of Jesus' disciples, desires a little assurance about Jesus' identity and asks Him to give them all a glimpse of the Father. Jesus takes the opportunity to convey to Philip that all along He's been showing them the Father through His own life and ministry. In short, Jesus was saying to Philip that He Himself was the perfect lens through which anyone could see the Father. As Philip no doubt pondered this glimpse into Jesus' own deity in relationship to God the Father, Jesus went on to challenge Philip's own recollection of how the Father's work was being performed in and through his life. And more, that the miracles Jesus performed would offer ample proof that, in being around Jesus, Philip and the rest of the disciples were in actual fellowship with His heavenly Father (John 14:11).

But then Jesus says another utterly amazing thing to Philip "I tell you the truth, anyone who has faith in me will do what I have been doing. He will do even greater things than these, because I am going to the Father. I will do whatever you ask in my name, so that the Son may bring glory to the Father. You may ask me for anything in my name, and I will do it" (John 14:12-14). Jesus is promising that when we ask for anything in His name, He will do it.

This needs a little explanation. Is Jesus promising, carte blanch, that whatever we want we get, as long as we ask for it in His name? Some TV evangelists would like to have us think so. They would have us think that as long as we are claiming something in Jesus' name, we can be assured it will eventually be ours; it's only a matter of time. I've met people who are just waiting for a piece of property to become legally theirs because they had already claimed it in Jesus' name. I don't mean to burst your bubble, but that's not what Jesus is promising here. Moreover, it's not what praying in His name actually means.

People who pray in Jesus' name often view that phrase much like a postage stamp that we place on a letter. They would suggest, "If we don't end our prayers with, 'In Jesus' name' our prayers won't get through." That kind of thinking, of course, is nonsense.

Here in John 14, Jesus is promising that there was a time when He would go back to the Father (John 14:12), at which time the Holy Spirit would be dispatched from the Father to indwell every true believer (Acts 1:8). What would follow? Greater works than even Jesus was able to perform.

But how? Certainly He wasn't suggesting we could multiply fish and loaves or raise the dead or turn water into wine, was He? No, He was simply saying that the Spirit that empowered Him to do these things would fill every believer so that they too might be able to do great works for God. Imagine every believer the world over being empowered and equipped to carry out great things for God! But how? Here's where prayer comes in. Jesus said, "I will do whatever you ask in My name, so that the Son may bring glory to the Father" (John 14:13).

We know we are asking in accordance with Jesus' instructions when our request is based on wanting Jesus to glorify the Father. This quickly eliminates all our self-centered and egotistical prayers concerned only for our own good or glory, not God's. This is what it means to be praying "in Jesus' name." If, however, we are asking for God to help us perform good works for His glory alone and the request would indeed bring glory to God, then we can be assured He will answer those prayers.

I got to know George when I was asked to visit his ailing wife who was reportedly on death's door. George wasn't a believer and to be honest, I don't think he liked me the first time I came to visit Mickey in their home. She was a believer in Jesus and loved that I had come to visit her. I could see that she liked that her husband had a chance to get to know me, too. Over time, my friendly visits softened George's heart as he welcomed me into their home. I could see God at work so

I prayed, not only for Mickey's life and future, but also for George's salvation.

For months I stopped by George and Mickey's home on my way from church after our Sunday services. I read Scripture to Mickey and prayed for her. Mickey lived for nearly a year after my first visit. By all accounts, this was a miracle in itself. Looking back, I believe God was answering prayers for Mickey by sustaining her health beyond what doctors had anticipated, so that George could hear the good news of the gospel and be saved. By the time Mickey passed into glory, George and I were clearly friends. He invited me to officiate at her funeral. There, at Mountain View Cemetery, George once again heard the message of the gospel.

In the weeks that followed, God put it on my heart to serve George. I began to do his yard work and odd jobs he needed done around his home. He didn't know this, but every time I mowed his lawn, or worked on a project for him, I prayed that God would help him see Jesus through me and see his need for Him. Sometimes we had little gospel talks; I went as far as George felt comfortable. One day, about 18 months after the death of his wife, George and I were standing on his porch. He thanked me for all the work I'd done for him for so long. "George, you know I love serving you. But even more, you know I pray that one day you will trust in Christ to forgive your sins and enter your life." I was stunned when he looked back and said, "I already have. A while back I gave my life to Jesus." What? I remember throwing my arms around him and saying, "That's awesome, George! Welcome to the family!"

George began attending church every Sunday he could. He sat down front and always made sure I saw that he was there as if to say to me, "I'm all in, Lar." George's baptism was beautiful. It was a true celebration. George's health eventually began to decline and a couple of years later, God welcomed George in His heavenly home. His daughter Ginny, who prayed more for her dad than I surely had, rejoiced knowing her father was now at peace. So much more could be said about my relationship with George. As I look back, I consider the "works" I was able to do for George to be exactly what Jesus promised in John 14, leading up to the ultimate work of God saving George from eternal separation from Him in Hell. The reason Jesus called these "greater works" is because believers around the world are performing faithful acts of love to countless millions of people in the hope that the gospel will be seen and heard with clarity. And it is! The church is exploding in so many places around the globe.

You see, our works are tied to our witness and prayer is an essential aspect of the process. I think this is what Paul had in mind when writing to the church at Colossae, "Devote yourselves to prayer, being watchful and thankful. And pray for us, too, that God may open a door for our message, so that we may proclaim the mystery of Christ..." (Colossians 4:2-3).

He continues, "Be wise in the way you act toward outsiders; make the most of every opportunity" (Colossians 4:5). Paul is reminding believers that our works are a means of witnessing and that prayer is needed throughout the process.

If we are keeping our eyes on Jesus, we should see each day as a season for doing good works. As we engage in these works, they become in some ways unconscious actions in response to the needs around us. In other words, we don't view people as "projects" or opportunities to leverage our agenda, no matter how noble it may be. I once heard pastor and author Tim Keller say, "We don't love people to share our faith with them. We share our faith and ourselves with them in order to love them." If we do, we'll be doing the greater works Jesus talked about.

Worry. Weakness. Doing good works. These are three seasons in which prayer can and should be utilized in our lives. Knowing these things is helpful but only if we put them into practice. Which area needs more attention in your life right now?

As we come to the end of this chapter and book, there are many aspects of prayer we've not examined or illustrated, such as praying for our enemies or prayers for personal repentance. We could have looked at the great priority of prayer in Jesus' life or in the life of the early church as recorded in the Book of Acts. We could have taken time to examine what Scripture says about things that hinder the effectiveness of our prayers. We could have cited examples throughout Scripture where people prayed under pressure and saw God do amazing things, as in the stories of Daniel, Job, Jonah, David, Nehemiah, the Apostles of Jesus and many others. Prayer is an exhaustible resource for every believer and its subject matter is found on most every page and book of the Bible. It's my hope that this brief exposition of the prayer Jesus taught his disciples, and these simple but practical words for putting prayer into practice, will encourage a greater passion for personal Scripture study about prayer and a greater engagement in practicing it unto the glory and praise of our great God and Savior, Jesus Christ.

DISCUSSION QUESTIONS

1. Of the three seasons mentioned in this chapter, which one do you relate to the most? Why?

2. In which season (worry, weakness or good works) do you feel you have grown the most in your walk with Jesus? What has been most helpful to your growth?

3. When, or in what situation do you feel most intimidated to pray about something? What have you learned in this chapter that you feel you can apply right now to help you be more confident when you pray?

4. Describe a time when God's peace followed a season of worry because you decided to pray about it.

5. What would you say to someone who thinks that prayer doesn't work because God hasn't given them what they are asking for?

6. Can you identify a time when God answered your prayer in a way you hadn't expected or even asked for? Share this with your group.

7. Take time to read aloud the three sections of Scripture explored in this chapter before having a short time of prayer for each other. (Philippians 4:6-7; Romans 8:26-27; John 14:12-14)

DR. LARRY A. VOLD

SENIOR PASTOR 3CROSSES

Dr. Larry A. Vold is Senior Pastor of 3Crosses in Castro Valley, CA. He earned a Masters in Theology from Simpson University and a Doctor of Ministry from Bakke Graduate University. Larry received Christ as a young boy and his life was transformed in high school thanks to a youth pastor who modeled what it meant to follow Jesus. He soon shared his faith with friends and witnessed to many at the Campus After Dark outreach.

Through these formational years, Larry experienced the power of God to help us all in both simple and profound ways and is steadfastly following Jesus and welcoming the Lord's grace in his life.

Pastor Larry is Chaplain for the Alameda County Fire Department. His interests include family time, basketball, bike riding and motorcycles, ocean fishing from his kayak and playing trumpet. He is also the author of *Know His Name*, available on Amazon.com.

RICK CHAVEZ - EDITOR

Rick Chavez enjoyed a successful career as a Bay Area TV/Radio anchor and voiceover talent, interviewing Hall of Fame athletes, Olympic champions and Silicon Valley executives. He was Sports Director at NBC11 in San Jose and anchored at ABC7 and KRON4 in San Francisco.

Rick hosted Cisco's first international SMB webcast from The Netherlands. In addition, he anchored Oracle webcasts in New Orleans and San Diego. Rick produced Silicon Valley tech reports for CNBC-Europe, was the host of *"Best of the Bay"* and won four Telly Awards for broadcast and documentary production excellence.

Rick was Jubilee Bible College Valedictorian in 2011 and now specializes in writing for Christian and Senior Living audiences. He is available to work with other authors as a freelance editor, proofreader or publisher. Please contact chavezmedia@gmail.com.

Made in the USA
Columbia, SC
08 March 2019